Positive Thinking

Published by
Lotus Press

Power of Positive Thinking

Anu Sehgal

Lotus PRESS
4263/3, Ansari Road,
Darya Ganj, New Delhi- 110002

Lotus Press
4263/3, Ansari Road, Darya Ganj, New Delhi- 110002
Ph.: 32903912, 23280047 • E-mail : lotus_press@sify.com
www.lotuspress.co.in

Power of Positive Thinking

ISBN: 978-81-8382-227-5
Reprint 2011

Published by : **Lotus Press,** New Delhi
Printed at : DD Offset Printing Press, Noida

Preface

Positive thinking, positive attitude and optimism are now known to be a root cause of many positive life benefits— the good life and well-being. You'll live longer and be healthier and happier with a positive attitude toward life. Positive thinking is a mental attitude that admits into the mind thoughts, words and images that are conductive to growth, expansion and success. A positive mind anticipates happiness, joy, health and a successful outcome of every situation and action.

Not everyone accepts or believes in positive thinking. Some consider the subject as just nonsense, and others scoff at people who believe and accept it. Among the people who accept it, not many know how to use it effectively to get results. Yet, it seems that many are becoming attracted to this subject, as evidenced by many books, lectures and courses about it. This is a subject that is gaining popularity.

The present book provides inspiring thoughts that will help you to create a positive change in your life. It will help you learn how to: build faith in yourself; cope with stress; get other people to like you; develop the power to reach your goals; eliminating negative thoughts that prevent you from achieving happiness and success and much more. It is hoped that the essence of this book will help readers to face the problems of daily life and to approach life positively.

-Author

Contents

1

What is Positive Thinking?

Positive thinking is a very simple concept that everyone can understand. Is the adoption of mental attitudes that makes anyone focus on certain thoughts and images that will help you achieve success, happiness and health. However sometimes is not that easy to actually do it when you are a negative thinker. But there are hundreds of people that have applied the principle of positive thinking and have had great success in their lifes. Having a positive mindset have given them the ability to achieve successful outcomes. On the other side, although millions of people have achieved great results applying the benefits of positive thinking over the years and also experts in medicine have proven that is very beneficial, there are still many people who believe that this concept is ridiculous. And there are also those who don't know how to apply positive thinking to their lifes although they know the concept. It can be due to inadequate commitment, but also because the negative thoughts, protect us and make us avoid rejection and failure.When we have this idea in our mind, changing from negative to positive thoughts is difficult, but can be done.

Positive thinking take us to through the way of achievement while negative thinking do the opposite by preventing us from succeeding. These becomes conscious and subconscious habits and patters that defines our personality.Most people that we deal with every day, tend to look for business partners, friends and anyone that has a positive attitude. And they try to avoid either conscious or subconscious people with negative thinking attitude. It becomes a challenge to change the way we think and make a personal commitment.Most people that are negative thinkers, don't know that they are negative thinkers and they also don't have idea of how to change that attitude. Obviously it has been long time that you have been thinking negative and will not be easy to change it quickly. To change your mindset from negative to positive you need complete commitment, inner change and understanding of your though process. However there is a lot of information available that you can acquire and learn it.

The first step is to understand and accept that a positive thinking mindset will lead you to success and the prove is that thousands of people who have done it use it. Some people have said that the power of positive thinking lies in its ability to give you happiness, satisfaction, health and business success. Many other have said that it changed their live after applying and expecting positive outlooks. There are many ways to look at this subject, however most medical experts and psychologists admit that, if you have a positive mind, it will be significantly for beneficial that being negative. Also a pleasant person is easier to deal with than a negative person that is always criticising and yelling everyone.

Its said that positive thinking can be contagious, if you are surrounded by positive people, you will sense their moods and respond accordingly, most people want to deal with a positive bright person. Also if you feel down and you are around positive people they can help you turn around your behaviour and smile to the situation.

Instead the negative person will make you feel worse. Its not difficult to think positively, all the great achievements in life have come from our conscious and subconscious mind. We are in charge to decide how we want to face things. You can change your attitude immediately. Most of our negative habits come from parents and teachers that were negative most of the time.

We have to challenge ourself to make a change and do whatever it takes to be positive, help people, acquire new positive habits and face problems with the right mindset. The power of the mind is immense, use it on your won benefit nor the contrary. Try it think positive and see the results that you will achieve in your personal life, health and business.

The Concept of Positive Thinking

The concept of 'positive thinking' is probably as old as human civilisation. But it emerged in an organised form, from Christian religious dissertations in early 1920s. When Joseph Murphy (1898-1981) wrote his famous "The Power of Your Subconscious Mind", he probably did not know how this psychological concept would be turned to a sociological phenomenon and resultantly, would be used politically. It did not take very long for the Vatican to base its texts and lectures by a host of religious figures, on the concept of 'No Negative thinking' and 'positive attitude'. These were the years of great depression in a democratic America. It seemed a very effective strategy to put a permanent stop on questions. See all positive. That was the potent message of that era. And then there was Second World War.

The father of the modern concept of Positive Thinking (PT), is Dr. Norman Vincent Peale (1898-1993). He came up with his best seller book *The Power of Positive Thinking* in a troubled post-WWII era. He had come from a religious background and made himself conspicuous for his religious works like *In God We Trust: The Positive Faith for Troubled Times" and "Faith is the Answer*. The state has made optimal use of clergy for manipulating people's collective thought. With love terrorism, so peculiar of religious elite of the time, Peale refuses to allow his reader to hear, speak and see an evil, and looking for only positivity in whatever they feel and see. His extensive lecture and seminars around the USA, were responsible for making positive thinking very popular and mainstream. His Centre for Positive Thinking carries an important work by disseminating excellent programmes that teach people how to achieve a positive mindset.

There were also several public speakers that took the concept to more popularity and it was mixed with religious discourses. There were also religious publications that touched on a positive mindset as a way to improve human growth and achievement, the most popular was the philosopher William James "Religion of Healthy Mindedness" published in 1902. And there were other people that used the concept of positive thinking in their lectures and sermons.

Positive thinking emerged from religious dissertations and came as a concept for personal improvement when Orison Marden published his success magazine in 1891. Emile Couse, referred him as the father of all inspirational thinking, but it is mainly credited for bringing positive thinking to the fore front as a self-help method in 1920s.

Power of Positive Thinking

Positive thinking is a mental attitude that admits into the mind thoughts, words and images that are conductive to growth, expansion and success. It is a mental attitude that expects good and favourable results. A positive mind anticipates happiness, joy, health and a successful outcome of every situation and action. Whatever the mind expects, it finds.

Not everyone accepts or believes in positive thinking. Some consider the subject as just nonsense, and others scoff at people who believe and accept it. Among the people who accept it, not many know how to use it effectively to get results. Yet, it seems that many are becoming attracted to this subject, as evidenced by the many books, lectures and courses about it. This is a subject that is gaining popularity.

It is quite common to hear people say: "Think positive!", to someone who feels down and worried. Most people do not take these words seriously, as they do not know what they really mean, or do not consider them as useful and effective. How many people do you know, who stop to think what the power of positive thinking means?

The following story illustrates how this power works:

Kiran applied for a new job, but as his self-esteem was low, and he considered himself as a failure and unworthy of success, he was sure that he was not going to get the job. He had a negative attitude towards himself, and believed that the other applicants were better and more qualified than him. Kiran manifested this attitude, due to his negative past experiences with job interviews.

His mind was filled with negative thoughts and fears concerning the job for the whole week before the job interview. He was sure he would be rejected. On the day of the interview he got up late, and to his horror he discovered that the shirt he had planned to wear was dirty, and the other one needed ironing. As it was already too late, he went out wearing a shirt full of wrinkles.

During the interview he was tense, displayed a negative attitude, worried about his shirt, and felt hungry because he did not have enough time to eat breakfast. All this distracted his mind and made it difficult for him to focus on the interview. His overall behaviour made a bad impression, and consequently he materialised his fear and did not get the job.

Rahul applied for the same job too, but approached the matter in a different way. He was sure that he was going to get the job. During the week preceding the interview he often visualised himself making a good impression and getting the job. In the evening before the interview he prepared the clothes he was going to wear, and went to sleep a little earlier. On the day of the interview he woke up earlier than usual, and had ample time to eat breakfast, and then to arrive to the interview before the scheduled time. He got the job because he made a good impression. He had also of course, the proper qualifications for the job, but so had Kiran.

What do we learn from the above story? Is there any magic employed here? No, it is all natural. When the attitude is positive we entertain pleasant feelings and constructive images, and see in our mind's eye what we really want to happen. This brings brightness to the eyes, more energy and happiness. The whole being broadcasts good will, happiness and success. Even the health is affected in a beneficial way. We walk tall and the voice is more powerful. Our body language shows the way you feel inside.

Positive and negative thinking are both contagious. All of us affect, in one way or another, the people we meet. This happens instinctively and on a subconscious level, through thoughts and feelings transference, and through body language. People sense our aura and are affected by our thoughts, and vice versa. Is it any wonder that we want to be around positive people and avoid negative ones? People are more disposed to help us if we are positive, and they dislike and avoid anyone broadcasting negativity.

Negative thoughts, words and attitude bring up negative and unhappy moods and actions. When the mind is negative, poisons are released into the blood, which cause more unhappiness and negativity. This is the way to failure, frustration and disappointment.

Positive thinking is the most important factor if you want to accomplish success in all areas of your life. Every time you think negative thoughts you have to change that thought into a positive and constructive one.

When you have a positive and constructive thought about your life you'll start feeling happier, more energised and the way you feel about the people around you will change for the better because you're looking at things from a different perspective. When you maintain this positive thinking people will feel good around you and will like to spend more time with you.

Every time you start to feel and think negative about something you have to turn that event around. Start thinking about new positive things. When you do this, your power of positive thinking starts working in your favour not against you.

The power of positive thinking is working in your favour. When negative memories come into your mind you have to say to yourself: "Every time I hold a negative event in my mind I'm attracting it into my life, so I'm going to focus on what's positive and important. That way I can attract more positive events in my life."

When you do this your mind starts to think positive thoughts. Always focus on how you can solve the problem not on the problem itself. Once you're aware of the power of positive thinking and start focusing on your desires, you begin to attract positive events that will help you manifest what you always wanted in your life.

Practical Instructions

The power of thoughts is a mighty power that is always shaping our life. This shaping is usually done subconsciously, but it is possible to make the process a conscious one. Even if the idea seems strange give it a try, as you have nothing to lose, but only to gain. Ignore what others might say or think about you, if they discover that you are changing the way you think.

Always visualise only favourable and beneficial situations. Use positive words in your inner dialogues or when talking with others. Smile a little more, as this helps to think positively. Disregard any feelings of laziness or a desire to quit. If you persevere, you will transform the way your mind thinks.

Once a negative thought enters your mind, you have to be aware of it and endeavour to replace it with a constructive one. The negative thought will try again to enter your mind, and then you have to replace it again with a positive one. It is as if there are two pictures in front of you, and you choose to look at one of them and disregard the other. Persistence will eventually teach your mind to think positively and ignore negative thoughts.

In case you feel any inner resistance when replacing negative thoughts with positive ones, do not give up, but keep looking only at the beneficial, good and happy thoughts in your mind. It does not matter what your circumstances are at the present moment. Think positively, expect only favourable results and situations, and circumstances will change accordingly. It may take some time for the changes to take place, but eventually they do.

Easier Approach to Positive Thinking

The power of positive thinking has long been held to be

a very important element in creating the kind of life you want. The benefits of positive thinking range from more happiness to how to attract abundance into your life, and everything else you desire.However, having daily positive thoughts is not the only thing that is important; it is also the positive feeling that we need to experience when we're doing the thinking. Our feelings add power to our thinking. Moreover, it is consciousness itself that is the source of both thoughts and feelings. So the power of positive thinking has its source in what is referred to as Being, or pure awareness.

The qualities of being are accessed and enlivened by allowing one's thinking to settle down to the point where awareness is simply aware, with nothing and no thoughts to be aware of. Therefore, the starting point for accessing the power of positive thinking is to access the power of the source of thinking itself—pure awareness—on a regular, daily basis. That alone will help to expand our consciousness so that more positive and life-supportive thinking results.

Positive Thinking Tips

Positive thinking is one of the most important things you need to practice throughout your life. When your attitude and behaviour are positive, you allow only pleasant feelings and constructive and positive thoughts to work in your mind. Although the mind is naturally predisposed to positive thinking, it doesn't like to change its thought patterns, and often subconsciously sabotages any attempts for looking on the bright side. The true power of positive thinking is that it allows you to live life to its fullest potential without letting negativity bring you down.

Positive thinking is a huge personal asset and the key to success. Changing your attitude to look at the positive side of every situation is the best thing you could ever learn to do. It is indeed refreshing to think positive in life. We all have lots of things going on in our lives and what we encounter day to day requires the right attitude to be able to make our lives happier and our goals easier to reach. Here are some little positive thinking tips to get you started.

1. *Be thankful.* Most often, we always look at what we do not have in life but it is hard for us to be grateful of what we have. There are a lot of things to be thankful for. If you did not get the promotion, be thankful you still have a job. Be thankful to the challenges in life, as it will help you live stronger. Being grateful, indeed, can turn the negative into positive—somehow it just a matter of looking at life a little differently.
2. *Believe in yourself.* Events and situations in life may not be the way you want them to be and some people may put you down and disappoint you, that is why you have to believe in yourself.
3. *Write positive affirmations to yourself and keep them.* Positive affirmations are powerful positive thinking tips that you can adopt in your life. You can write them into a paper and keep them. This way, you are overpowering and slowly eliminating the many negative thoughts that have been buried in your subconscious for many years.
4. *Write all negative thoughts you have and burn them.* If you have a bad habit of saying negative things to yourself or if you often have negative thoughts about something, write it down and burn them.
5. *Give yourself positive thoughts in front of the mirror.* One of the many positive thinking tips you can do is to do positive affirmation in front of the mirror. Tell yourself statements that will help you think positively about yourself.

6. *Don't let negative people influence your thoughts.* These people will pull you down and tell you that you cannot do this or that. If not, they will tell you of problems that will soon happen to you. They will only discourage you with negative thoughts and statements that will only push you to doubt yourself. Your choice then is to avoid these kinds of people or do not let their discouraging words put you down. Go with people who are positive about life and you will also be positive about life. These attitudes are contagious, thus be careful who you are going with.
7. Think positive thoughts about any situation in the different aspects of your life.
8. Get in the habit of surrounding yourself with positive people because this will help you to be more positive. If you have ever spent much time around a negative person they can really drag you down.
9. Start spending time in a positive environments because your environment helps to set the tone for how you think and feel.
10. Be aware of how you feel and think and be willing to change your attitude thoughts when they are negative. The most highly successful people keep close tabs on their thoughts because they know the importance of positive thoughts and how they play a key roll in getting things done.
11. Read more positive uplifting stories. This will inspire you and feel better about yourself and your life. Try to make it a habit of reading some positive material at least half an hour a day.

So if you want to change the way you look at things and live life positively, you can start with these positive thinking tips. By learning how to be positive with your thoughts, you will eventually realise how good it is to think positively and live life positively.

Understanding Negative Thinking

People often don't know how to stay positive in the face of what they experience in their lives. And if you've ever known a depressed person, or have experienced depression yourself, you'll know that it is not an easy thing to swing around from that feeling to one of positive thinking.

In fact, jumping from depression to lightness, happiness and positivity in an instant is pretty much impossible. The leap is just too much of a jump. The shift can, however, be taken in smaller steps, by fostering new habits of using your attention.

So-called negative people can indeed become more positive. The best way to start the journey from negativity to positivity is to start the journey towards more happiness.

In terms of thinking, speaking and human attitudes, there is probably a generally held yet rather vague idea of what the word 'positive' means, and what we mean when we use the term, the power of positive thinking.

Positive thinking refers to the kind of thinking that causes one to have good feelings. For example, good feelings could include optimism, certainty, exhilaration, friendliness, love, happiness, joy, admiration, acceptance, peace and so on.

On the other hand, a negative thinker would experience different kinds of feelings—feelings that are not so pleasant, such as pessimism, doubt, resistance, a critical view of things, an argumentative stance, unfriendliness, not being liked or loved, unhappiness, fear, and so on.

The power of negative thinking is just as awesome as the power of positive thinking. What we give our attention to, and how we habitually think about things, can create the very things we don't want.

The term the power of positive thinking may leave one with the impression that only positive thinking is powerful, because it can bring us the life situation we desire and all the good stuff the abundance gurus talk about. However, the truth is that all thinking—and attitude, attention and feeling—is powerful, because what we give our attention to is what we enliven in our own lives. So, while not being a positive thinker will certainly stop the good things from showing up in our lives, thinking negatively is just as powerful. But it brings to us the kinds of things we don't want—whether it be people, situations, sickness, being mugged, unhappiness, or anything else we'd rather not have in our lives.

Become friends with the power of positive thinking and deliberately and consciously turn away from the power of negative thinking.

Our attention and our thinking enliven whatever we consistently focus on, which is then drawn to us—by us. We do it ourselves, by courtesy of the way our universe works. Positive thinking draws the good stuff. And through the power of negative thinking we draw to us the opposite. It's our own choice which one we want to have as our continual habit.

Values of Positive Thinking

Successful thinking is a Mindset possessed by some of the greatest athletes, politicians and business people in history and modern day times. Some examples of successful thinking and positive mindset that come to mind are Donald Trump, who has been bankrupt three times, and Bill Gates, founder of Microsoft.

Successful people act as though they have accomplished or are enjoying something. Soon it becomes a reality. Successful people often find themselves in situations where risk and uncertainty is hanging over them and if they were to take on a negative mindset then failure would rear its ugly head. Instead high achievers embrace risk and uncertainty in difficult situations and keep a positive outlook. Nine times out of 10 usually end up with the results that they had in mind all along.

Positive attitude is extremely important, as it encourages individuals to approach each day, and each problem, with a bright outlook. In a team environment, a positive attitude encourages a team to work together with individual styles and personalities. Positive attitude is not only about choosing to have a good outlook through good times and bad, but also about learning to love what you do. Outstanding business people are successful because they deeply love their work.

All of our feelings, beliefs and knowledge are based on our internal thoughts, both conscious and subconscious. We are in control, whether we know it or not. We can be positive or negative, enthusiastic or dull, active or passive. The biggest difference between people is their attitudes. For some, learning is enjoyable and exciting. For others, learning is a drudgery. For many, learning is just okay, something required on the road to a job.

Our present attitudes are habits, built from the feedback of parents, friends, society and self, that form our self-image and our world-image. These attitudes are maintained by the inner conversations we constantly have with ourselves, both consciously and subconsciously. The first step in changing our attitudes is to change our inner conversations.

One approach is called the three C's: Commitment, Control and Challenge.

- *Commitment.* Make a positive commitment to yourself, to learning, work, family, friends, nature, and other worthwhile causes. Praise yourself and others. Dream of success. Be enthusiastic.
- *Control.* Keep your mind focused on important things. Set goals and priorities for what you think and do. Visualise to practice your actions. Develop a strategy for dealing with problems. Learn to relax. Enjoy successes. Be honest with yourself.
- *Challenge.* Be courageous. Change and improve each day. Do your best and don't look back. See learning and change as opportunities. Try new things. Consider several options. Meet new people. Ask lots of questions. Keep track of your mental and physical health. Be optimistic.

Studies show that people with these characteristics are winners in good times and survivors in hard times. Commitment, control and challenge help build self-esteem and promote positive thinking. Here are some other suggestions.

- In every class, look for positive people to associate with.
- In every lecture, look for one more interesting idea.
- In every chapter, find one more concept important to you.
- With every friend, explain a new idea you've just learned.
- With every teacher, ask a question.
- With yourself, keep a list of your goals, positive thoughts and actions.
- Remember, you are what you think, you feel what you want.

Having a positive attitude starts with the unfolding of the largely untapped potential of our own creative consciousness, which we can consciously access at the point where the mind is silent yet awake.

Millions of people around the world engage in one of other form of meditation to access the quiet consciousness within. If you're not yet one of those, then you have to seriously consider taking up such a daily practice. Search for information, ask others, get recommendations, and find some effective meditation techniques to choose from—methods that take the mind beyond the surface level of thinking and simply culturing peaceful moods, to increasingly quieter states of functioning.

Successful positive thinking is a mindset possessed by some of the greatest athletes, politicians and business people in history and modern day times. Some examples of successful positive thinking and positive mindset that come to mind are Donald Trump, who has been bankrupt three times, and Bill Gates, founder of Microsoft.

Successful people act as though they have accomplished or are enjoying something. Soon it becomes a reality. High achievers embrace risk and uncertainty in difficult situations and keep a positive thinking.

Positive thinking and positive attitude is extremely important, as it encourages individuals to approach each day and each problem, with a bright outlook. In a team environment, a positive attitude and thinking encourages a team to work together with individual styles and personalities. Positive thinking is not only about choosing to have a good outlook through good times and bad, but also about learning to love what you do.

2

Mind, Body and Power of Thought

The mind plays an important role in achieving every kind of success and goal, minor, everyday goals or major goals. With minor or day-to-day goals, one usually knows what he wants to do or get, but when it comes to major goals, most people don't know what they really desire. They desire to do something big, but they don't know what. You may have a vague idea, but this is not enough. To accomplish anything, and to use your mind power, you have to know exactly what it is you want to do. To focus your mind power on a goal, you need to have a clear and well defined goal. How do you go about that?

You have first to think or meditate, to find out what is it that you want to accomplish or gain. For this, you need focused and clear thinking. This ability can be improved and strengthened by practice. After discovering what you really want to accomplish, you need to come up with a plan for action. You need to know what you have to do first and how to proceed. All of this requires planning, which means using the power of the mind.

After deciding on a goal and coming up with a plan, you need to hold in your mind a clear mental image of your goal. You need to see it accomplished. This step requires that you use your imagination, which is another power of the mind. Not everyone can visualise clear mental images, but regular training of the imagination can do wonders. You may, for example, look at photos of what you want to achieve, and then close your eyes, and try to see it in your imagination. This will enhance your ability to visualise. At this point you have to display patience, self-discipline and the power to persist in your efforts. This requires a one pointed mind.

Affirmations are another useful mental tool for you to use. What you affirm sinks into the subconscious mind, becomes part of the subconscious mind, and consequently affects your behaviour and actions. If your affirmations are positive, they lead you to success.

Another important power of the mind is thought transference. You need to be able to transmit your thoughts to other people, who would aid you with your plans. Often, you have to persuade others to invest in your plans or to help you in other ways. It is not enough just to talk with them, you need to believe in what you are saying; you need to be enthusiastic and persuasive, otherwise they won't listen and won't care. You need to be able to reject your and their doubts. To be able to do so, you need concentration, control over your thoughts, will-power, self-discipline and patience. All these are mental tools and skills.

Motivation is another mental and emotional power that you require. How can you achieve anything if you are not motivated enough? To increase your motivation and enthusiasm, think often of your goal, about its advantages and benefits, and how it will change your life. Doing so, will strengthen and your motivation.

Your thoughts, which are part of your mind, possess power. The thoughts that you most often think tend to come true. If you pour your mental energy into the same thoughts or mental images day after day, they will become stronger and stronger, and would consequently affect your attitude, expectations, behaviour and actions. These thoughts and mental images can even be subconsciously perceived by other people, who would then offer you help or opportunities. Your thoughts can also create what is usually termed as coincidence. They can attract into your life corresponding events, situations and opportunities.

IMPORTANCE OF MIND POWER

Mind power is the second strongest power next to the spirit. The thoughts that pass through your mind are responsible for everything that happens in your life. Your predominant thoughts influence your behaviour and attitude and control your actions and reactions. As your thoughts are, so is your life.

You have to be careful of what you think. Thoughts are like a video cassette that is played in the VCR of the mind. What you play is what you see and experience. What you think is what you live. To make changes in your life it is necessary to eject the old video cassette, and insert a new one that you like.

The power of thoughts is creative. It is possible to train and strengthen it. With it you can cause your thoughts to manifest on the material plane, and you can influence other people's minds.

If you give seeds water and fertilisers they grow into healthy and strong plants. Thoughts, like seeds, have a natural tendency to grow and manifest on the material level if they are fed with attention and interest.

Your thoughts pass to your subconscious mind, which in turn influences your actions in accordance with these thoughts. Your thoughts also pass to other minds, and consequently people who are in a position to help, give you their help, sometimes without even knowing why. The power of your mind is part of the creative power of the Universe, which means that your thoughts work together with the mighty Universal mind. Using effectively the power of thoughts can be termed "practical day-dreaming".

Visualise a perfect scene of whatever you want to accomplish. Put a lot of detail, colour, sound, scent and life into these mental scenes. Repeat them often, with faith and attention, and the subconscious will accept them as real experiences. It does not differentiate between real and imaginary experiences, and accepts them both as real.

Actions, situations and objects that you visualise frequently eventually manifest on the material plane in a natural way. It is as if new software has been installed in the mind, and which affects the outer world. This manifestation does not happen overnight. It needs time, and depends on how ambitious and sincere you are, and how much time and attention you put into this action.

This process can be used for changing, improving or developing any kind of habit, ability or skill, and it is useful for gaining money, possessions and promotion, for building a business, improving health and relationships, changing circumstances and for practically almost everything. Pay attention to the thoughts you think. Learn to let into your mind only the thoughts that bring good, happy and positive results.

Power of Imagination

Imagination is the ability to form a mental image of something that is not perceived through the senses. It is the ability of the mind to build mental scenes, objects or events that do not exist, are not present or have happened in the past. Memory is actually a manifestation of imagination. Everyone possesses some imagination ability. In some it may be highly developed and in others it may manifest in a weaker form. It manifests in various degrees in various people.

Imagination makes it possible to experience a whole world inside the mind. It gives the ability to look at any situation from a different point of view, and enables one to mentally explore the past and the future.

It manifests in various forms, one of which is daydreaming. Though too much idle day-dreaming may make one impractical, some day-dreaming, when not being engaged in something that requires attention provides some temporary happiness, calmness and relief from stress.

In your imagination you can travel anywhere in the speed of light without any obstacles. It can make you feel free, though temporarily, and only in the mind, from tasks, difficulties and unpleasant circumstances.

Imagination is not limited only to seeing pictures in the mind. It includes all the five senses and the feelings. One can imagine a sound, taste, smell, a physical sensation or a feeling or emotion. For some people, it is easier to see mental pictures, others find it easier to imagine a feeling, and some are more comfortable imagining the sensation of one of the five senses. Training of the imagination gives the ability to combine all the senses.

A developed and strong imagination does not make you a daydreamer and impractical. On the contrary, it strengthens your creative abilities, and is a great tool for recreating and remodelling your world and life.

This is a great power that can change your whole life. It is used extensively in magic, creative visualisation and affirmations. It is the creator of circumstances and events. When you know how to work with it, you can make your hearts' desires come true.

Imagination has a great role and value in each one's life. It is much more than just idle day-dreaming. We all use it, whether consciously or unconsciously, in most of our daily affairs. We use our imagination whenever we plan a party, a trip, our work or a meeting. We use it when we describe an event, explain how to arrive to a certain street, write, tell a story or cook a dish.

Imagination is a creative power that is necessary for inventing an instrument, designing a dress or a building, painting a picture or writing a book. The creative power of imagination has an important role in the achievement of success in any field. What we imagine with faith and feelings comes into being. It is the power beyond creative visualisation, positive thinking and affirmations.

Visualising an object or a situation, and repeating often this mental image, attracts the object or situation into our lives. This opens for us new, vast and fascinating opportunities.

This means that we should think only in a positive manner about our desires, otherwise we may create and attract into our lives events, situations and people that we don't really want. This is actually what most of us do, because we don't use the power of imagination correctly. If you do not recognise the importance of the power of the imagination, and let it run riot, your life may not be as happy and successful as you would have wanted it to be.

Lack of understanding of the power of the imagination is responsible for the suffering, incompetence, difficulties, failures and unhappiness people experience. For some reason, most people are inclined to think in a negative way. They do not expect success. They expect the worst, and when they fail, they believe that fate is against them. This attitude can be changed, and then life will improve accordingly.

Understanding how to use your imagination correctly, and putting this knowledge into practice, for your own and others' benefit, will put you on the golden path to success, satisfaction and happiness.

Imagination and Inner Vision

Imagination, which can also be called inner vision, is a gift that has many positive applications, but more than often it is not well-developed or correctly used. Few people possess the ability to control what enters their minds. They let their minds and imagination do as they please, and let any stray thought or mental image appear on the screen of their inner vision. This lack of control leads to lack of control over their lives.

Let your imagination run riot, and your life will be a mess. Control it and visualise only what you intentionally decide to visualise, and you change your life in accordance with your will.

What is the imagination, the inner vision? It is the ability to see in one's mind mental images of something that exists, and also the ability to imagine objects, situations or circumstances that do not exist now. Imagination is not only visualising mental images. It is possible to visualise using all the five senses. You can visualise a sound, taste, smell or a sensation. If you watch your mind, you will find out that you are constantly using your imagination in various ways. You use it while thinking about the past or future, planning, painting, writing, and describing something. You use it when you describe how to get to a certain street, when you read and when you day-dream.

Do you write, paint or engage in any creative activity? Do you cook, decorate or love to do new things? If you do, then you are using your imagination. When you worry or feel fear you use it too. At such times you automatically visualise unhappy or unfortunate situations. If you keep visualising these negative mental images you may eventually attract them into your life.

If you see in your inner vision how you want your life to be, and continue watching this mental scene every day with faith, concentration and love, one day your life will look exactly as you imagine.

There are some people who say they have no imagination. There is no such thing. It may be weak, but they certainly possess it. It might also happen that their visual imagination is not strong, but they can visualise using their other five senses, as mentioned earlier.

The ability to visualise clearly can be developed, and this can be fun. Exercises for developing this ability will at the same time also improve your ability to concentrate, and as a bonus, you might find that you gain a power which you can use to shape and improve your life.

Developing the imagination, the power of your inner vision:

— Find some fifteen minutes every day for the exercises.

— Visualise something simple that you can believe you can get, such as going to a movie with your friend or with your husband/wife, eating at a certain restaurant or doing something else you would like to do.

— Visualise your desire clearly, and include in the visualisation all the five senses. If it is watching a movie together with another person, imagine the two of you entering the cinema and sitting down.

Listen to the people around you, use your sense of smell and feel the coldness or warmth in the cinema hall. Visualise eating popcorn or drinking some soft drink, and enjoy the taste and smell.

- You might find out it is easier to imagine with some of the senses, and a little difficult to imagine with the others. Go on with the exercises and you will strengthen your ability to imagine with all the senses.
- Do the same exercise everyday, and you will find that it gradually becomes easier.
- Sometimes you may find that your mind starts to verbalise about what you are imagining. Be careful not to replace the imagination with words. The aim is to use the imagination, not words.

If you follow these suggestions you will develop your imagination, the power of the inner vision, which will be useful to you in many situations. You might also be surprised to discover that what you see in your mind, in your inner vision, comes true in real life.

Becoming the Boss of Your Mind

Most people keep thinking the same kind of thoughts, and visualise the same mental images in an unconscious automatic manner. This means they keep viewing the same movie in their minds, and consequently go on creating and living the same kind of life.

You can change the thoughts and images in your mind, which is equivalent to inserting a new cassette into the VCR of the mind. As thoughts create events and circumstances, by changing the habitual thoughts, life's events and circumstances change too.

Most people don't know or don't believe that it is possible to change their way of thinking. The reality of this possibility has never occurred to them.

There are people who have the knowledge and make the effort. If they persist in their efforts to become more conscious of their thinking process, and attempt to control and filter the contents of their minds, they realise in a practical and direct way that their thoughts are creative and possess power.

Silencing the mind is a higher stage that very few know about, and fewer take practical steps to achieve. If and when one reaches this goal he realises that he is not his mind or his thoughts, but something beyond. He realises and experiences in a very clear and direct manner the reality of his True Essence, and the illusion of what is called "reality".

The ability of silencing the mind is the key to the switch of the mind, enabling us to turn it on and off as we wish. When we are able to switch it off at will, we experience serenity of mind, strength, confidence and happiness. When the mind and its thoughts are quiet, we are able to use the mind in a most effective way.

Silencing the thoughts and the incessant, tiring, consuming chatter of the mind makes us enjoy a peaceful and joyous consciousness. At this stage we become the boss of the mind.

A strong power of concentration makes it easier to free the mind from thoughts. When there are no thoughts to distract, one becomes fully aware and conscious of the true eternal inner being. This is the goal of spiritual seekers, yogis and saints. This is the secret goal beyond every tradition and religion. This secret is yours to live and enjoy, if you strive towards it.

The mind is responsible for everything that happens. It is the creator of everything in the world. The world is dependent on the mind for its existence. When in deep sleep with no dreams, are you conscious of the world? Is someone in a swoon, conscious of the world? No, consciousness of the world happens only when the mind is active. In deep meditation, when the mind is quiet the world seems to disappear.

When you master your mind, you master your world. When you are able to silence the mind, you free yourself of negative habits and attitudes. Then the mind cannot influence the way you feel, your moods, and your behaviour.

When you can silence the mind, at least for a while, you realise that you are not the mind. It is a sort of energy that occupies your attention incessantly. For someone who encounters this approach for the first time, it may sound weird and silly. Someone who has practiced meditation for some time, or is conversant with the Eastern philosophies will understand and accept these words. From this inner silence you can look at the mind, understand what it is and come to know its nature and how and why it works.

While working towards this inner state, the mind usually suggests all kinds of reasons and excuses why it is better not to bring it under control. It wants to be free and roam wherever it likes. It believes that if it is silenced, life will cease to be. It cannot accept that life can go on without its incessant chatter and inner dialogues. It is false logic, as the mind cannot know what is beyond it. The moment it is silenced it does not participate in what happens after this silence. Then how can it experience a state in which it is absent? It cannot think about a state it has never experienced.

There is no vacuum in nature. When the mind is made quiet, something "new" steps in. It is the Universal Consciousness, Spirit, the creative power, your "inner I", you can call it whatever you want. It is a power that has always existed, it is in us, it is us. It is our true Consciousness, which we have forgotten.

Power of Thoughts

If you keep thinking about difficulties, fears and failure your life will mirror these thoughts. If you keep thinking about your current circumstances you will keep recreating them. Most people get caught in this way of thinking, and consequently attract into their lives the same kind of events and circumstances over and over again.

You can change your thoughts and choose the thoughts you want. This will change your life. You can right now start to think in a different way and paint new, beautiful, and positive images in your mind. You can refuse to look at the old pictures and scenes that fill your mind. You can look at the mental pictures of your choice, even if your actual circumstances are very different from these mental images.

You have a projection room in your mind, and you can choose which film to play. In the inner room of your mind you can hang the pictures and paintings of your own choice. Does a feeling of power surge through you now, as you read these lines.? You can master your life!

Thoughts are the inner strings that pull circumstances and situations. You can be the one pulling theses strings and make your life happier and more satisfying. When you are the boss of your mind you have the power to improve your inner and emotional life, relationships and your material and financial status.

Some make a mediocre change; some go the extreme and become leaders in politics, education, finance or any other field. Your ability, and how far you go is dependent on how free you are from being the slave of the mind and subject to its tyranny, and the extent of your ability to choose your thoughts and change the contents of your mind.

It is possible to go even further then this, though few do. There are some who aspire to reach the source of the mind and find the switch that turns it on and off. This is the switch of true inner freedom. When they succeed, they realise the secret that many have sought down the ages. They find the silence beyond thoughts, the real freedom.

Becoming the boss of your mind enables you to think about what you want, when you want to. You stop being influenced by outside forces, and become a partner in the creation of your life.

When you rise above your mind, you will be able to recognise it as it is, a tool for your use. You will arrive to a point, where you will be able to free yourself from its dictates. This may ultimately lead you to experience a higher state of consciousness, about which all the spiritual traditions of the world have always taught about, and towards which they pointed.

Types of Inner Powers

We all possess various inner powers, but they are often in a dormant state. In order to awaken these inner powers and start using them, special training and inner work is required. Sometimes, due to various unpredicted circumstances, some of these powers might manifest unexpectedly and temporarily. What are these inner powers? Let's review them briefly:

Power of Concentration

This is the ability of focusing the attention on one single

object or thought, and at the same time excluding all other unrelated thoughts from the mind.

Concentrating on one single thought or subject directs the mental energies into one point and prevents their dissipation. Concentration strengthens the power of the thought focused on, and can achieve wonders. This action is similar to the action of a magnifying glass that concentrates the rays of the sun into one single beam, and which can then burn a piece of paper. This ability can be developed through special exercises. Any time spent on such exercises is time well spent. The more time and energy you devote to strengthening the power of concentration, the stronger this ability becomes.

Willpower

This is the inner strength to make decisions, take action and handle and execute any aim or task, regardless of inner resistance, discomfort or difficulty. It manifests as inner firmness, decisiveness, determination, resolution and persistence.

Self-discipline

This inner power manifests as the ability to forgo instant gratification in favour of something better, and of the giving up of instant pleasure and satisfaction for a higher goal. It is the ability of the individual to stick to actions, thoughts and behaviour, and which leads to improvement and success.

Power of Imagination

This is the ability to experience a whole world inside the mind. Imagination is a creative power. By training and using it correctly one can create and attract health, wealth, happiness and favourable events and circumstances.

Imagination is not limited only to seeing pictures in the mind. Feelings and sensations relating to all the five senses can be imagined too. It is possible to imagine sounds, tastes, scents, physical sensations, feelings and emotions.

A well-developed and strong imagination does not make one a day-dreamer or an impractical person. On the contrary, it strengthens the creative abilities, the ability to solve problems and is a great tool for recreating and remodelling one's life and circumstances.

This is a great power that can change one's whole life. It is used extensively in magic, creative visualisation and affirmations. The power of the imagination creates and transforms circumstances and events. When you know how to work with it you can make our hearts' desires come true.

Persistence

It is so easy to stop and give up when one's plans don't turn out as expected or take too much time to accomplish. Persistence manifests as the inner strength to continue in spite of difficulties, obstacles and failure.

Motivation

Motivation is an inner driving force, which directs one toward a chosen aim or goal. In order to accomplish anything, one needs a driving, directing power, otherwise nothing would happen, and motivation supplies this power.

Ambition

Wishful thinking is not strong enough to make one take action. A wish is a weak desire. Only a strong desire can drive one forward, to take action, follow plans and accomplish desires and goals.

Self-confidence

This is faith in one's abilities, strength and power. Confidence leads to courage, doing things, trying new things and to success.

Detachment

This is the ability to remain calm and uninvolved on the emotional and mental levels. This ability saves one a lot of trouble, discomfort, fears and worries. Detachment helps one to accept calmly what cannot be changed and go on with one's life. Detachment leads to inner balance and peace.

Peace of Mind

A peaceful mind is free from the compulsion of incessant and restless thinking and worrying. When thoughts do not disturb the tranquillity of the mind one experiences inner happiness. A person possessing peace of mind is calm and in control of himself. Such a person retains inner balance under almost all conditions, and is hardly affected by negative circumstances and situations.

Can you imagine a successful person, who cannot concentrate on a task, hasn't the willpower to follow his or her goal or is unable to visualise the kind of success he or she desires to attain?

Can anyone reach high spiritual levels without concentration, will power and self-discipline?

Even people who pursue psychic or occult training need the above-mentioned inner powers.

Do you wish to follow a particular course of action, change habits, lose weight, learn a new skill, study or succeed in your examinations?

Do you desire to develop psychic powers, clairvoyance or telepathy?

Do you want to excel in creative visualisation?

Whatever is your aim in life is, all of the above mentioned inner powers are of great importance and should be developed and strengthened.

Psychic Powers

Every person displays or experiences some psychic power every now and then, though most often these experiences are dismissed as pure coincidence. You certainly have had some premonitions about something that was going to happen, dreams that came true, or you felt and knew what someone was thinking of you. These experiences often came spontaneously, suddenly, and without any prior preparations.

Some people are more naturally psychic from others, and psychic experiences are a more common occurrence with them. Sometimes they just accept the fact that they are a bit different from others in their perceptions, having as if a sixth sense, while others pursue the subject more deeply, reading, learning and searching for guidance. They try to develop these powers and bring them under their control.

Psychic powers can be developed through special training, even by people who are not naturally psychic. These are fascinating powers, which allow a trained person to peek beyond the material plane, and know things that remain hidden to other people.

There are several risks in using and developing psychic powers, which one has to take into account when developing them:

1. The knowledge gained can be used for selfish purposes.
2. The psychic could be wrong in interpretation of the experience, and might unintentionally mislead, misguide or cause harm to other people.
3. Some of the psychic powers requires one to be mentally passive, so as to be able to tune in to other minds, thus letting in some external powers, which might have a negative influence.
4. One who is not well-balanced and lacks self-control and discipline, might find it difficult to stop the psychic impressions and lead a practical normal life.
5. Pursuing psychic training might deter one from the path of self-improvement and spiritual growth, leading him or her to constant seeking of these perceptions and leading away from inner calmness and peace of mind.

If one desires to develop psychic powers, it would be wiser first to develop some concentration ability, control over the mind, willpower, self-discipline, mental & emotional detachment. This would ensure that one be able to open and close at will the mental doors, and so avoid being influenced by what he/she perceives. This will also reduce the danger that one might misuse the powers or get his/her ego inflated by them.

There are different kinds of psychic powers or gifts, as they are often called. Another term used is ESP—extrasensory perception. Here is a list of some of the psychic powers:

1. *Clairvoyance (clear vision)*: Seeing far away scenes and places or hidden things, without using the physical eyes. Clairvoyance enables one to perceive scenes and mental images with the mind's eye.

2. *Clairaudience (clear hearing)*: Perceiving sounds or words from a distant or from other realms. Clairaudience enables one to hear words and sounds not perceived by the physical ears.
3. *Clairempathy (clear emotion)*: Sensing the attitude or emotions of another person.
4. *Psychometry*: Perceiving information about a person, place or an object, by holding in one's hands an object belonging to the person or place. In Psychometry one usually holds some small personal object such as a watch, ring, key or other personal object.
5. *Psychokinesis*: The ability to move objects through the powers of the mind.
6. *Intuition*: Perceiving an idea, knowledge or information directly. This is what is commonly called "a gut feeling". Intuition is some kind of inner knowledge and certainty about something.
7. *Telepathy*: Reading other people thoughts and sending them your thoughts.
8. *Mental influence*: An advanced kind of telepathy that allows one to influence the minds of other people.
9. *Psychic healing*: The ability to cure pains or illnesses by transferring some kind of healing energy.
10. *Auric sight*: The ability to see or sense the colours of the aura, and thereby understand certain things about the moods, emotions, thoughts or health of other people.

Mind Power and Prosperity

Prosperity and success can be yours if you seek them with an open mind. Find out your inhibiting thoughts, analyse them and learn to get rid of them. Put into your mind positive and unlimiting thoughts, visualise your desire day after day, and gradually you will start to see your circumstances improving.

Thoughts possess great power. You should be aware of the thoughts you think and admit only positive ones. If you desire prosperity and riches, admit only these thoughts into your mind. Learn to free your mind from limiting thoughts as suggested earlier, and then use the power of your mind to attract success into your life.

Visualisation is one of the most important keys to success. Visualise clearly your desire, put feelings into your mental images, add faith and belief, and you have created a mighty power. Keep an open mind, be willing to act and take up the opportunities that will come your way, and you are on the proper road to success.

Attaining Unlimited Wealth

The word wealth brings into the mind thoughts about riches, plenty of money and the ability to buy and enjoy whatever one wants. It brings thoughts about fancy houses, hotels, world travel, cars and everything money can buy. It is something most people want, but do not believe they can get and enjoy.

Wealth is all the above and much more. It is not restricted only to money and possessions. It manifests as plentitude in various and many forms in our life and in nature. A person can be wealthy with love, compassion, goodness, strength, energy, knowledge and wisdom. Nature manifests wealth in the many life forms and plants it produces, and in the endless stars and worlds it has created.

The life force, which is also called the universal consciousness, spirit or creative power, desires to constantly express and manifest itself, and it does so through the physical frame of plants, animals and human beings. This power also expresses its desire to manifest wealth, which is the desire to grow, develop and become stronger and bigger. Yet, many find this desire and natural tendency for growth inhibited in them, due to negative programming, negative thinking and lack of faith in themselves and their abilities.

The first step to make wealth flow into your life is to change your thoughts and attitude toward it. The mind has to be cleared from its wrong concepts about wealth, before it can start to manifest. This is done by bringing to consciousness all of your thoughts and ideas about wealth, money and prosperity.

Take a pen and a sheet of paper, and find a place to be alone and undisturbed for a while. Think about wealth and what it means to you, and then jot down any thought that comes into your mind. Write down every thought, good and bad, positive and negative. Do this for at least ten minutes or until you do not find more ideas and thoughts.

After you finish writing, read, think, and analyse what you have written. You will be surprised at the stuff that comes out of your mind. This analysis will help you to find out where and why you are inhibiting yourself in regard to success, money, and prosperity. You will find out what thoughts and wrong concepts have been holding you back.

You will discover the fears that have been holding you from success, and from manifesting any degree of riches in your life. There might be various reasons to account for that. You may have been educated to regard wealth as bad and corrupting. You may have experienced lack in your childhood, and now you are locked into the belief that it is not possible to improve your life or that you do not deserve to possess money.

It might be that you shun the responsibility and the work that wealth might entail. Maybe you are afraid that you would not be able to handle wealth or that you will not know what to do with it. These reasons or any others might be responsible not experiencing prosperity and wealth. The inner inhibitions are mostly due to former mental programming, making you feel and believe that you are not worthy, do not deserve success or that wealth and money should be avoided.

If you perform this analysis sincerely, you will find out what thoughts and attitudes hinder your way to success, and it will be clearer to you what you should do. Now that they are out, it will be easier to handle these inhibitions, free yourself from their grip, and to start attracting wealth into your life. If one session is not enough, keep writing down your thoughts, and think about them every day until feel you have discovered what is holding you back.

After this analysis you will find it easier to start changing your thoughts and attitude towards money, possessions and wealth. You will find it easier, and experience less inner resistance when you visualise what you want to get or accomplish. It will take less effort to refuse negative or contradictory thoughts from entering your mind. Persistence in your efforts of holding an image of success in your mind until you realise your desire, and at the same time keeping an open mind for opportunities will lead you to do the right thing at the right time, and attract the right people at the right time.

An intense and concentrated thought possesses a vast power. All wealthy people focus their energies in a positive and powerful manner on what they desire to achieve. Some of them understand and practice consciously the laws of success, while others do so unconsciously.

The universal consciousness is unlimited and contains unlimited wealth. There is plenty of everything in it, and it constantly creates more of everything. It expresses itself through everything, including the individual unit that you consider as yourself. The problem is that negative thoughts and attitudes hamper the natural tendency of the universal consciousness to freely manifest its creative powers in unlimited ways.

You need to open your mind to prosperity and throw away your limiting thoughts. It does not matter how limited your life and circumstances are at the present moment, because if you choose to change your thoughts and attitudes, and start thinking without imposing limitations, your life will start to change. In your mind, refuse to be tied and limited by your circumstances. Think about possibilities, not about limitations.

Expand your unlimited thinking to what you consider as yourself, your personality and individuality. Your consciousness is one with the universal consciousness. If you consider yourself as only a body you limit yourself. You are limitless consciousness, but erroneously identify yourself with the body and therefore feel limited. The feeling of limitation obstructs you from expressing the great powers of the universal consciousness. By being one with the universal consciousness you participate in the power of creation. Think about it, you are connected to the powers of the universe.

In your search for wealth it is important not to be too attached to it. If you heed this suggestion you will save yourself a lot of trouble. Pursue wealth and material objects if and when they are necessary and add ease and happiness to your life, but do that without attachment.

By expressing detachment, you become able to avoid frustration, depression and anger if things do not turn out as expected. Material objects come and go. It is only temporarily that we own them. Attachment to possessions brings fear, anger and feelings of insecurity. On the other hand, detachment concerning possessions makes us feel free, and helps us to view the material life in a saner and more practical way.

Detachment is not indifference. It is a feeling of inner freedom and strength. If you develop this quality you will be able to stay composed and in control of yourself in every situation. This quality will also help you make new starts if things do not go well, without brooding over the past.

3

How to Maintain Positive Energy?

The concept of positive thinking and affirmations is a popular topic throughout the media and mainstream self-improvement channels. We will discuss how intentional modifications of thought processes actually help us to improve quality of living.

Thoughts can be viewed as a system of processing information and extracting neural data from our memory stores. For most people, very few thoughts actually coincide with the action that is occurring in the present. The mind is wandering and distracted by thoughts of the past or the future. These waves of irrelevant thoughts can be easily tainted with negative attributes fuelled by the Ego: anger or resentment from past interactions, jealousy or envy from unfulfilled desires, worry or anxiety from future events. By addressing these negative thought patterns and modifying the resulting manifestations, we can avert a cascade of negative energy on the body and mind.

When the mind is saturated with negative thinking, these thoughts gradually manifest into the physical as dysfunction. Negative thoughts are often accompanied by stress. The brain releases specific stress-response hormones to facilitate reactions in body necessary to react to this stress. If the negative thoughts and stress remain constant, these hormonal reactions generate chronic strain on the organs and physical systems.

By tuning into our response systems, we can clearly recognise the signs of this harmful cascade of negative energy. We can experience many health conditions like muscle tension, headaches, poor sleep and fatigue, poor digestion, weight gain, high blood pressure and circulatory problems, poor breathing patterns, and organ dysfunction like diabetes.

Instead of waiting for these negative health conditions to arise, we can monitor our thought patterns through the other path of manifestation—our emotions. Our inner and outer emotions immediately reflect our current thought patterns and are an indication of eventual physical manifestations.

Impact of Positive Energy Life

The law of attraction states that we transmit positive and negative energy constantly. Others pick up on positive energy and gravitate towards us or pick up on negative energy and are repelled by us. Positive energy can help you achieve your goals.

How do you know if you're emitting positive energy? The best—and easiest—way to know is by looking at the people in your life. Are they encouraging and uplifting, or are they draining away your energy?

You're emitting positive energy when you:

— Stay in touch with your dark side and weaknesses, and are willing to grow towards healing and strength. Positive energy is about movement.

— See the positive qualities in other people. Positive energy values other positive qualities.

— Feel compassion towards yourself and the world.

- Listen to—and try to understand—other perspectives, regardless of how different. Positive energy is open minded.
- Give the benefit of the doubt. Positive people don't judge quickly.
- Express your true-self in thoughts and actions, gently and honestly. Positive energy is honest.
- Share your negative thoughts and emotions. Positive energy admits the negative.
- Celebrate the success and happiness of other people. Positive energy appreciates success.
- Feel fear and defeat, and keep persevering anyway. Positive energy doesn't deny negative emotions.
- Follow your dreams and desires.

You're not emitting positive energy when you:

- Ignore your dark side and weaknesses (and then act them out). Negative energy isn't up front.
- Focus on other people's mistakes and weaknesses. Negative energy is critical.
- Obsess about being perfect; whether it's at work, at home, or with your appearance. Negative energy strives for perfection.
- Try to change other people's perspectives and opinions. Negative energy wants everyone to be of one mind.
- Try to please people constantly and ignore your own needs. Negative energy isn't balanced.
- Let other people's moods and energy dictate your own.
- Swallow your negative thoughts and emotions.
- Resent the successes and joys of others. Negative energy is jealous.

— Allow fear and cynicism to harden your heart and colour your perspective. Negative energy revolves around fear and bitterness.

— Ignore your goals, plans, and passions. Negative energy suffocates your dreams.

People with positive energy are determined to do their best, and to see the best in the world around them. People with positive energy don't focus on "should have" or idealised, perfect expectations that are impossible to live up to. People with positive energy have an open heart and a sense of humour. People with positive energy don't care about being popular or keeping up with the Jones' and they stay in touch with their hearts and souls. People with positive energy achieve their goals.

People with positive energy make mistakes and own up to them. They keep lines of communication open, opting for discussion and connection—and people with positive energy are satisfied with "agreeing to disagree." Failures and disagreements don't face people with positive energy, because they know they're part of living and working with humans!

Positive Thought Energy

Every thought you think is created by choice or habit Every thought you think creates your health and circumstances! Really think about that, You chose your thoughts and therefore create your circumstances! This is an astoundingly simple and powerful way to improve your life. Did you know that blissful joy is your natural state of being? We just "learn" to be negative as we grow through life. We initially learn our thinking patterns as children from our peers, so by the time we are adults our thought patterns are more or less set... Unfortunately however there seems to have been very little importance placed on the great significance of thought energy in the past. This means most of us are living with habitual thought patterns that can keep us stuck in non exciting dull lives. We may dream about living a wonder filled life, but most of us never dare to think it's really possible.

One of the most important part of this to accept is that you are much, much more than just a physical body, we are all, each one of us, magnificent source energy beings, here in this physical world for the fun of it! We have just got a little lost along the way as we fret about life.

It is scientifically proven that

- Every thought you think is created by choice or habit.
- Each thought you think has a frequency that can be scientifically measured.
- Everything within our whole universe is made of energy, from the stars in the sky to the molecules that make you.
- Your thoughts and feelings are also energy and they attract like energy.
- Therefore each thought we think, has an effect on our reality.

What you repeatedly focus your attention on, one way or another ends up in your reality. You attract to you what you allow your mind to dwell on. The stronger your emotion is on the subject you are thinking about, and the longer you dwell on it, the more "pulling power" it has in creating your experience and health. So, in other words every thing you are experiencing now you have actually drawn to you. Accepting this is the beginning to generating a life of health, bliss and abundance. Especially, since you now know you can choose your thoughts and therefore create a reality you really want to live in.

How to Change Your Thought Patterns?

Firstly, it is important to note that a positive thought is 100 times stronger that a negative one so don't worry about any negative thoughts you have been pampering, just read on. One of the ways to easily change your thought patterns is by being aware of how you feel. When we feel negative; i.e. angry, resentful, jealous, etc. that's the trigger for you to decide to change.

The next time you catch yourself worrying or thinking negatively about something, just calmly take a step back and decide to think about the situation differently, with the knowledge that you can Choose your thoughts and feelings, repeat a positive, present tense thought in place of the negative one. Choose an Affirmation, like " All is Well in My World" Simply repeat this over and over, put real feeling into this new thought, choose to feel good! Really it's that simple; You are guaranteed to feel better about your "negative issue" almost immediately.

However, to really make a difference you need to be dedicated and use your affirmation every time you feel yourself slipping back into your negative thought pattern again, it takes 30 days to change a habit, thought habits included, so just stick with it—practice with patient persistence. At first it will feel as if you are deceiving yourself, but in a short time you will start to come into alignment with your new thought, you will start to come into alignment with your true self! and that my friend is when the magic starts to happen.

While practising give yourself time to really absorb your new chosen positive thought, until you create a positive feeling that resonates throughout your body. You may not be able to reach a blissful feeling the first few times but you can defiantly achieve a better feeling than the negative one you have been dwelling on. By putting good feeling into your affirmation you will maximise the effect and begin to create yourself a life of positive situations and circumstances.

Most of us are unaware that by simply learning to master our thoughts we can radically change our lives...but believe me you can, we can all do this and it is simple, you just need to Practice with Patience Persistence! As you begin to transform yourself into a positive person by changing your thought patterns you will no longer attract negative people or situations. You will find unexpected pleasures adorn your days; where there was once negativity or melancholy there will be fun, smiles and joy.

Practising with Positive Thought Energy

One of the strongest times of day to practice this, is as you awake first thing in the morning; you know that semi sleep dreamy state, It can take a little practice however to catch yourself in dream like state before you become fully awake. Again just practice with Patient Persistence.

If you have a situation at hand that is affecting you in a negative way, or even a meeting coming up that you are concerned about. Use the time as you awake or fall asleep to imagine the situation unfolding in the most positive way possible, play with it dwell on this beautiful positive outcome.

Another fantastic way to change your thought patterns is by writing your new positive thoughts or affirmation 20 times a day; 10 times in the morning and 10 times at night, (more if you want!) By physically writing down your new positive thought you much more focused on it, making the whole change take place even quicker. If you can sing your new thoughts in a song or ditty it has a stronger effect too!

Its not enough just to think these thoughts, you have to put feeling into them too, and it is the very best positive feeling you can muster. The universe responds much better, much faster to strong good Feeling Thought. When you are feeling positively ecstatic about something you almost tingle, right? Think about the last time you felt that way? Maybe when you received good news, held someone you love, when you were somewhere you could really relax, find a memory that generates that fantastic feeling of bliss.

So now you have a picture in your mind of something that makes you feel good—hold onto the feeling, discard the actual specifics of the memory, what you want to do is dwell on the blissful feeling. Let yourself generate and hold this feeling whenever you want, so when you are practising your positive present tense thought you can really charge it with this positive feeling. You can even imagine sparkles of energy dancing in and around these new thoughts if you want to, really go to town with this, its power is incredible.

Keeping these new positive thoughts in the present tense is very important. It's not positive thoughts of "what is going to be" that will make any changes. If your new thoughts are in a repeated future tense, then that's exactly where your changes will take place—sometime in the future—always out of reach.

Coverting Negative Energy to Positive Energy

Achieve your goals by creating positive energy and making positive thoughts work for you. Changing your negative energy into positive thoughts will help you achieve your goals. Create positive thoughts by integrating these habits into your life. Some ways to make positive thoughts work for you are given below:

1. *Catastrophising.* "If I don't ace this presentation, I'll get fired." Your habit is to predict the absolute worst outcome; everything is a potential disaster. "Everything will be ruined if they don't show up on time." Every mole is a sign of cancer, every headache a brain tumour. Those are not positive thoughts that will help you achieve your goals.

   Make thoughts positive by letting it go. A positive thought is: If you don't ace the presentation, you'll be like everyone else—nobody always performs perfectly! Maybe you didn't get the data on time, maybe you're overtired because you have a new baby. Doesn't matter because if you don't give a perfect presentation every time you probably won't lose your job. As for "Everything will be ruined if they don't show up on time"—what's your definition of *ruined*? The rice isn't hot? The birthday boy isn't surprised? Ruined is car crashes and trees falling on houses, it's not people showing up late. Make positive thoughts work for you by looking at the big picture.

2. *Discounting the positive.* "This old thing? It has a stain I'll never get out. I bought it years ago at Value Village, it makes me look fat." Similar to using a negative filter, you shrug off the positive and focus on the negative. "She's only saying that because she has to." Those are not positive thoughts that will work for you.

   Make thoughts positive by focusing on the positive. When someone compliments you, revel in the feeling. Preen! Even if she's only saying it because she "has to" (which of course you don't know)—who cares? Enjoy feeling flattered, and shrug off that negative energy. Positive thoughts will help you achieve your goals.

3. *Mind reading.* "I don't care what you say, I know what you're thinking. You think I'm stupid!" "They all hate me." You think you know what others are thinking or feeling, regardless of what they say. This is negative energy that blocks positive thoughts.

   Make thoughts positive by accepting your humanity. You don't know what others are thinking. Listen to what they say with their words and body language; do they really think you're stupid? Do they really hate you? It's doubtful. Ask what they really think—and believe their answer. Let go of negative energy and make positive thoughts work for you.

4. *Predicting the future.* "We'll never get to the airport on time. We'll miss our flight!" You think you know what will happen, and it's not usually good. "I know I won't get the job because I asked about the photo on the desk during the interview. She'd never hire such a nosy person!" This is negative energy that will create a self-fulfilling prophecy.

5. *Exaggerating.* "Sure I was hired—but now look at the seven hour commute I'll be facing every day. Great." You assign more importance to negative energy and give positive thoughts less importance. "We had a fight and now we're headed for divorce!" Your negative energy is a depressing filter. Positive energy and positive thoughts will refresh and revitalise you.

Suggestions to Support Positive Energy Level

When our emotions turn negative, heavy, and burdensome, we can stop, take a deep breath and simply reflect. What has generated this emotion? What thought has taken hold to create this toxic mental state? By just reflecting, we often observe this thought (and emotion) dissipate and loose its' hold on the mind and body. Through practice and discipline, we can more readily remain in a *sattvic state* (one of harmony, calm, and presence).

Here are some suggestions in supporting the practice of positive thought generation:

— *Address your environment and the stimuli that are entering the mind.* Avoid places and interactions that are filled with negative energy. Newspapers, gossip columns, and radio/TV news thrive on negativity. Surround yourself by a network of positive-minded people. Reduce your interaction with relationships that foster thoughts and actions that flow against your positive intentions.

— *Start and end your day with a simple pause allowing time to reflect on appreciation.* Take note of several things you are truly thankful for. Sincere expression of appreciation is a powerful tool to facilitate positive thought processes and generate a sense of fulfilment in the moment.

— *Speak only when it improves upon silence.* This subtle, yet powerful Buddhist phrase says it all. Speech is another physical manifestation on thought. Controlling our words trains our thought processes. If a conversation can not be steered to a positive tone, end the conversation.

— *See the world with less judgement.* Judgement is another toxic element of negative thinking. Practice finding "good" in everything. Experience the freedom of releasing established biases and expectations. Often when we judge, we too have issues with being judged. A non-judging mind becomes free of the "eyes" of the outside world and we begin to live within ourselves and not through others.

— *Engage in lifestyle habits that support healthy thinking.* Regular exercise, proper rest, meditation, proper nutrition plans, and uplifting activities help keep the mind fresh and expressive with positive energy. Also consider how you can modify your work environment with changes like taking more consistent breaks to proper work ergonomics.

— *Get things done and organised.* Just as thoughts manifest into the physical, the physical environment manifests back into the mind. Finish incomplete projects. Organise your home and workspace. An environment that is unorganised or filled with incomplete tasks has a burdening effect on the nervous system. Declutter and make your environment flow with spacious, positive energy. Clean out closets and cupboards so the first and last thing you see in the day is organisation and order. This physical order supports mental calmness and control of emotions.

Rather than trying of purge negative thoughts, focus more on generating positive interactions and expressions. This aspect of sankulpa (the practice of establishing an intention) attracts further positive thoughts and experiences. With this shift into harmonious thinking, the physical manifestations are seen and experienced by others. We begin to attract more people with like minds and intentions. Again, the key element is reflection and observation. What are our emotions saying about our thoughts? Use your emotions as a tool. Breathe new life in your thinking and experience the freedom of positive thought energy.

Ideas for Keeping your Positive Energy

Some ideas for keeping your positive energy flowing are given below:

1. Remember that your thoughts create your destiny. Recognise your own power to create your life.
2. Stop worrying. Often by worrying we feel like we are "doing" something about a problem when we aren't. When we worry we are in the past or in the future. By staying in the present we can actually problem-solve the situation as it actually exists.
3. Don't believe in defeat. Unexpected opportunities often come with what initially seem like negative outcomes or mistakes. Also, when you feel defeated, make a list of the factors that are supportive of you, rather than focusing on those that are against you.
4. Stop all those little negatives because they grow in to large ones. Use thought stopping and the steps toward changing your negative self-talk.
5. Name what is blocking your positive thoughts. What prevents you from thinking positive all the time?
6. Examine each of your core beliefs in terms of how it operates in your life. Make a commitment to yourself to eliminate the ones that cause you distress or problems.
7. Focus on the present. Your energy is drained by regretting the past and worrying about the future. Stay grounded in the here-and-now where it is easier to actually problem—solve the real situations.
8. When faced with a problem, focus on possible solutions and the resources that you do have. Brainstorm. What are the many options available, not just the black-and-white solutions or obvious ones?

9. Take self-responsibility. Stop blaming others for your unhappiness. Recognise the consequences of your choices.
10. Identify your personal definition of success. This helps you decide which path you want to take and to know when you have arrived at your goal. Your definition of success will be unique to you. No one else can define it for you.
11. Fill your life with positive supportive people. Allow their positive opinion of you in. Don't block them because their opinions do not fit your image of yourself. What is the worse thing that could happen if you thought positive thoughts about yourself? You might actually feel more energetic and motivated and have more fun!
12. Avoid draining your energy by focusing on the past and looking at mistakes that have already been made. Focus on the lesson learned and not on the mistake. What can you learn from the choice you made, whether it was a good choice or not?
13. Express your appreciation and positive feelings toward others. Say thank you when they complete simple daily tasks. Avoid draining your energy focusing on what they didn't or haven't done.
14. When feeling overwhelmed by change, make a list of what is staying the same and what is not changing. What do you already know? What can you keep doing the same as before?
15. Acknowledge out loud your positive traits and successes. Question why it is considered conceited or arrogant to talk about what you do well.
16. Keep a gratitude journal. Each night before bed list three things that you are grateful for that day. Some days it may simply be that you are grateful that the day is finally over!

17. Work at being content with who you are rather than pleasing others by wearing your social mask. When you wear a mask and try to be everything to everyone it can be exhausting. There is no space left for you.
18. Ask yourself: "How do I manufacture my own unhappiness?"
19. Keep asking yourself what is really important. In five years how much will this really matter?
20. Brainstorm a list of what makes you happy. Direct your attention to what pleases you. How can you allow or create more of this in your life?
21. Practice random acts of kindness.
22. Suspend judgement of yourself and others. Practice self-acceptance and acceptance of others. What does judging yourself or someone else achieve? Acceptance does not mean never changing. However, you cannot change what you don't recognise or accept you are doing.
23. Affirm and reaffirm your assets. List ten achievements you have obtained over the last five years. It could be finding a new job, taking a course, learning a new skill or changing your attitude.
24. Trust your intuition. Your intuition is that "gut feeling" or that hunch. It is your inner self speaking to you.
25. Create a home environment that is pleasing and nurturing to you.
26. Work at a job that energises you.
27. Slow down. Learn to respond, rather than react.
28. Our own attitude is often what we see reflected in others. People in our lives act as mirrors to allow us

to see ourselves more clearly. If you are surrounded by negative people, take a look at yourself. How might these people be a reflection of your own attitude? Similarly, as you become more positive you will attract more positive people to you. Initially though, as you become more positive the negative people in your life may escalate their negatively in order to try to pull you back in. Remember it is not your job to change them. Focus your energy on being more positive and creating more positive energy in your own life.

4

Positive Thinking for Stress Management

Stress is factor in every person's life. Stress from family matters, financial problems, work related, stress caused by illness and pain, sexual dysfunction, and environmental stress are the most common forms of stress that affect people. Finding ways to reduce stress can better your health in many ways. Different things work for different people but there are a few things that every person can do to relieve stress and better there life. Positive thinking helps greatly with stress management and can improve your health. Pessimism is very common and many have a hard time over coming it. You can overcome negative talk by recognising it and practising some techniques that overcome it. By learning to put positive thinking into action it will not only relieve stress but it will help you live a happier life as well.

Some of the benefits from positive thinking are decreased stress levels, boost your immune system, sense of well being, reduced risk of heart disease, easier breathing if you have emphysema, and improved coping abilities. Self-talk is the endless stream of thoughts that run through your head every day. These thoughts in your head can either be negative or positive and some of it comes from logic or reason and others from lack of information that is misconceptions. If most of the thoughts that run through your head are negative your outlook on life is mostly pessimistic. If they are positive thoughts then your outlook is mostly optimistic.

Some ways to know if you are a pessimistic person is to write down your thoughts through out the day. Then look back on them. Do they sound gloomy and dreadful? Most people magnify negative aspects of situations and filter out the good things. Or when something bad happens a person automatically blames themselves and thinks that its their fault. Automatically anticipating the worst is very common as well.

Instead of giving into these kinds of talk set aside misconceptions or irrational thinking and challenge them with rational positive thoughts. The process is simple but it takes time and lots of practice. Don't forget you are trying to create a new habit while get rid of an old one.

Randomly threw out the day stop and evaluate what you are thinking about, if you find they at negative find a way to put a positive spin on them. Start by telling your self you're not going to say anything to your self that you wouldn't say to anyone else.

Some examples are "it's too complicated" instead tell yourself "I will tackle it in a different way". "There's not enough time" instead tell yourself "lets re-evaluate some priorities" or "it's too big of a change" instead try "let's take a chance". Very simple things like this can make all the difference on stress and your life.

Practising positive self-talk will improve your outlook nut don't expect to change overnight. Over time you will automatically contain less self-criticism and have more self-acceptance. It will also make you less critical of the world around you. When you are thinking in a positive way you make yourself able to handle everyday stress in a conductive way.

Another thing you can try for relief from stress is a product from Alternative Health Supplements. Stress Release from Bell is a formula that gives back the nutrients that the body needs when it is stressed out and it helps to calm the nervous system. It also works on the production of hydroxyl that commands the central nervous system and encourages the production of serotonin in the brain. This product will also help the adrenal glands when the body and brain are under attack from stress. Combining this product with the use of positive thinking will be a sure fire way to put a stop to overloading stress in your life.

Stress—Underlying Mechanisms

There are two types of instinctive stress response that are important to how we understand stress and stress management: the short-term "Fight-or-Flight" response and the long-term "General Adaptation Syndrome". The first is a basic survival instinct, while the second is a long-term effect of exposure to stress. A third mechanism comes from the way that we think and interpret the situations in which we find ourselves. Actually, these three mechanisms can be part of the same stress response—we will initially look at them separately, and then show how they can fit together.

"Fight-or-Flight"

Some of the early work on stress established the existence of the well-known fight-or-flight response. His work showed that when an animal experiences a shock or perceives a threat, it quickly releases hormones that help it to survive. These hormones help us to run faster and fight harder. They increase heart rate and blood pressure, delivering more oxygen and blood sugar to power important muscles. They increase sweating in an effort to cool these muscles, and help them stay efficient. They divert blood away from the skin to the core of our bodies, reducing blood loss if we are damaged. And as well as this, these hormones focus our attention on the threat, to the exclusion of everything else. All of this significantly improves our ability to survive life-threatening events.

Unfortunately, this mobilisation of the body for survival also has negative consequences. In this state, we are excitable, anxious, jumpy and irritable. This reduces our ability to work effectively with other people. With trembling and a pounding heart, we can find it difficult to execute precise, controlled skills. And the intensity of our focus on survival interferes with our ability to make fine judgments based on drawing information from many sources. We find ourselves more accident-prone and less able to make good decisions.

It is easy to think that this fight-or-flight, or adrenaline, response is only triggered by obviously life-threatening danger. On the contrary, recent research shows that we experience the fight-or-flight response when simply encountering something unexpected. The situation does not have to be dramatic: People experience this response when frustrated or interrupted, or when they experience a situation that is new or in some way challenging. This hormonal, fight-or-flight response is a normal part of everyday life and a part of everyday stress, although often with an intensity that is so low that we do not notice it.There are very few situations in modern working life where this response is useful. Most situations benefit from a calm, rational, controlled and socially sensitive approach.

General Adaptation Syndrome and Burnout

Hans Selye took a different approach from Cannon. Starting with the observation that different diseases and injuries to the body seemed to cause the same symptoms in patients, he identified a general response (the "General

Adaptation Syndrome") with which the body reacts to a major stimulus. While the Fight-or-Flight response works in the very short term, the General Adaptation Syndrome operates in response to longer-term exposure to causes of stress.

Selye identified that when pushed to extremes, animals reacted in three stages:

- First, in the Alarm Phase, they reacted to the stressor.
- Next, in the Resistance Phase, the resistance to the stressor increased as the animal adapted to, and coped with, it. This phase lasted for as long as the animal could support this heightened resistance.
- Finally, once resistance was exhausted, the animal entered the exhaustion phase, and resistance declined substantially.

Selye established this with many hundreds of experiments performed on laboratory rats. However, he also quoted research during World War II with bomber pilots. Once they had completed a few missions over enemy territory, these pilots usually settled down and performed well. After many missions, however, pilot fatigue would set in as they began to show "neurotic manifestations". In the business environment, this exhaustion is seen in "burnout". The classic example comes from the Wall Street trading floor: by most people's standards, life on a trading floor is stressful. Traders learn to adapt to the daily stressors of making big financial decisions, and of winning and losing large sums of money. In many cases, however, these stresses increase and fatigue starts to set in.

At the same time, as traders become successful and earn more and more money, their financial motivation to succeed can diminish. Ultimately, many traders experience burnout.

Stress and the Way We Think

Particularly in normal working life, much of our stress is subtle and occurs without obvious threat to survival. Most comes from things like work overload, conflicting priorities, inconsistent values, over-challenging deadlines, conflict with co-workers, unpleasant environments and so on. Not only do these reduce our performance as we divert mental effort into handling them, they can also cause a great deal of unhappiness. The most common currently accepted definition of stress is something that is experienced when a person perceives that demands exceed the personal and social resources the individual is able to mobilise.

In becoming stressed, people must therefore make two main judgements: firstly they must feel threatened by the situation, and secondly they must doubt that their capabilities and resources are sufficient to meet the threat. How stressed someone feels depends on how much damage they think the situation can do them, and how closely their resources meet the demands of the situation. This sense of threat is rarely physical. It may, for example, involve perceived threats to our social standing, to other people's opinions of us, to our career prospects or to our own deeply held values. Just as with real threats to our survival, these perceived threats trigger the hormonal fight-or-flight response, with all of its negative consequences.

Stress and Your Health

We've already looked at the survival benefits of the fight-or-flight response, as well as the problems this caused for our performance in work-related situations. We've also seen the negative "burnout" effect of exposure to long-term stress. These effects can also affect your health—either with direct physiological damage to your body, or with harmful behavioural effects.

Behavioural Effects of Stress

The behavioural effects of an over-stressed lifestyle are easy to explain. When under pressure, some people are more likely to drink heavily or smoke, as a way of getting immediate chemical relief from stress. Others may have so much work to do that they do not exercise or eat properly. They may cut down on sleep, or may worry so much that they sleep badly. They may get so carried away with work and meeting daily pressures that they do not take time to see the doctor or dentist when they need to. All of these are likely to harm health.The direct physiological effects of excessive stress are more complex. In some areas they are well understood, while in other areas, they are still subject to debate and further research.

Stress and Heart Disease

The link between stress and heart disease is well-established. If stress is intense, and stress hormones are not 'used up' by physical activity, raised our heart rate and high blood pressure put tension on arteries and cause damage to them. As the body heals this damage, artery walls scar and thicken, which can reduce the supply of blood and oxygen to the heart. This is where a fight-or-flight response can become lethal: Stress hormones accelerate the heart to increase the blood supply to muscles; however, blood vessels in the heart may have become so narrow that not enough blood reaches the heart to meet these demands. This can cause a heart attack.

Other Effects of Stress

Stress has been also been found to damage the immune system, which explains why we catch more colds when we are stressed. It may intensify symptoms in diseases that have an autoimmune component, such as rheumatoid arthritis. It also seems to affect headaches and irritable bowel syndrome, and there are now suggestions of links between stress and cancer. Stress is also associated with mental health problems and, in particular, anxiety and depression. Here the relationship is fairly clear: the negative thinking that is associated with stress also contributes to these.The direct effects of stress in other areas of health are still under debate. In some areas diseases traditionally associated with stress are now attributed to other causes. Regular exercise can reduce your physiological reaction to stress. It also strengthens your heart and increases the blood supply to it, directly affecting your vulnerability to heart disease.

Stress and Your Performance

So far, we have seen that stress is a negative experience. We have seen the short-term negative effects that stress hormones can have on your performance, and have seen how stress can contribute to burnout. Sometimes, however, the pressures and demands that may cause stress can be positive in their effect. One example of this is where sportsmen and women flood their bodies with fight-or-flight adrenaline to power an explosive performance. Another example is where deadlines are used to motivate people who seem bored or unmotivated.

In most work situations jobs, our stress responses causes our performance to suffer. A calm, rational, controlled and sensitive approach is usually called for in dealing with most difficult problems at work: Our social interrelationships are just too complex not to be damaged by an aggressive approach, while a passive and withdrawn response to stress means that we can fail to assert our rights when we should.Before we look further at how to manage stress and our performance, it is important to look at the relationship between pressure and performance in a little more detail, first by looking at the idea of the "Inverted-U", and second by looking at

"Flow". This is the ideal state of concentration and focus that brings excellent performance.

Pressure and Performance

The relationship between pressure and performance is explained in one of the oldest and most important ideas in stress management, the "Inverted-U" relationship between pressure and performance. The Inverted-U relationship focuses on people's performance of a task.

The left hand side of the graph is easy to explain for pragmatic reasons. When there is very little pressure on us to carry out an important task, there is little incentive for us to focus energy and attention on it. This is particularly the case when there may be other, more urgent, or more interesting, tasks competing for attention.

As pressure on us increases, we enter the "area of best performance". Here, we are able to focus on the task and perform well—there is enough pressure on us to focus our attention but not so much that it disrupts our performance.

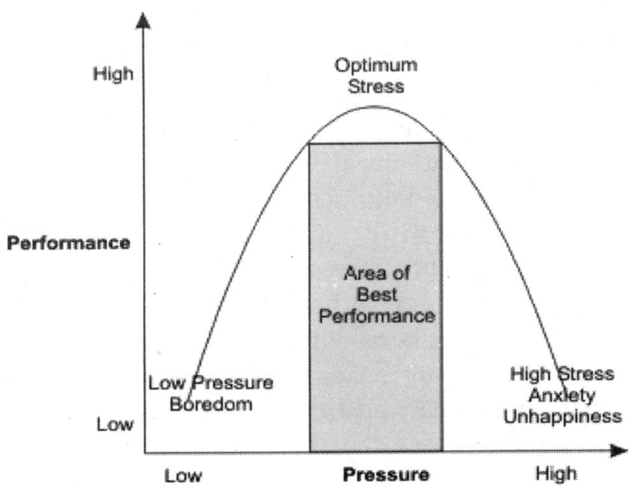

Figure 1: Inverted-U relationship between pressure and performance

NEGATIVE THOUGHTS CROWD OUR MINDS

We are all aware that we have a limited short-term memory: If you try to memorise a long list of items, you will not be able to remember more than six or eight items unless you use formal memory techniques. Similarly, although we have huge processing power in our brains, we cannot be conscious of more than a few thoughts at any one time. In fact, in a very real way, we have a limited "attentional capacity".

As we become uncomfortably stressed, distractions, difficulties, anxieties and negative thinking begin to crowd our minds. This is particularly the case where we look at our definition of stress, i.e. that it occurs when a person perceives that "demands exceed the personal and social resources the individual is able to mobilise." These thoughts compete with performance of the task for our attentional capacity. Concentration suffers, and focus narrows as our brain becomes overloaded.

As shown in the figure, this is something of a slippery slope: the more our brain is overloaded, the more our performance can suffer. The more our performance suffers, the more new distractions, difficulties, anxieties and negative thoughts crowd our minds.

Other research has shown that stress reduces people's ability to deal with large amounts of information. Both decision-making and creativity are impaired because people are unable to take account of all the information available. This inability accounts for the common observation that highly stressed people will persist in a course of action even when better alternatives are available. It also explains why anxious people perform best when they are put under little additional stress, while calm people may need additional pressure to produce a good performance.

While this is an important and useful idea, people's evaluations of stress and performance are by necessity subjective. This has made it difficult to prove the 'Inverted-U' idea formally. Also, for ease of explanation, we show a smooth curve here. In reality, different people have different shaped and positioned inverted-Us at different times and in different circumstances. This is all part of "life's rich tapestry".

Entering a State of Flow

When you are operating in your "area of best performance", you are normally able to concentrate, and focus all of your attention on the important task at hand. When you do this without distraction, you often enter what Professor Mihaly Csikzsentmihalyi of Chicago University describes as a state of 'flow'. This involves "being completely involved in an activity for its own sake. The ego falls away. Time flies. Every action, movement, and thought follows inevitably from the previous one, like playing jazz. Your whole being is involved, and you're using your skills to the utmost".

You perform at your best in this state because you are able to focus all of your efforts, resources and abilities on the tasks at hand. While you are sufficiently motivated to resist competing temptations, you are not so stressed that anxieties and distractions interfere with clear thought. This is an intensely creative, efficient and satisfying state of mind. It is the state of mind in which, for example, the most persuasive speeches are made, the best software is developed, and the most impressive athletic or artistic performances are delivered.

One of the frustrations of management is that managers can feel that they lose the 'right' to these periods of deep concentration when they must be readily available to others, and be able to deal with the constantly changing information, decisions and activities around them. Studies of good managers show that they rarely get more than a few minutes alone without distraction. This alone can be frustrating, and can contribute strongly to managerial stress.

In jobs where concentration is a rare commodity, there are various solutions to creating the periods of flow that sustain good performance. Solutions include working from home, or setting aside parts of the day as quiet periods. Another solution might be to delegate the activities that require the greatest levels of concentration, allowing the manager to concentrate on problems as they arise, serving to create a flow of its own.

Stress Management

Our main definition of stress is that stress is a condition or feeling experienced when a person perceives that demands exceed the personal and social resources the individual is able to mobilise. With this in mind, we can now look at how you can manage all of the stresses that your career will bring. From our definition, you can see that there are three major approaches that we can use to manage stress:

— *Action-oriented*: In which we seek to confront the problem causing the stress, changing the environment or the situation. To be able to take an action-oriented approach, we must have some power in the situation. If we do, then action-oriented approaches are some of the most satisfying and rewarding ways of managing stress. These are techniques that we can use to manage and overcome stressful situations, changing them to our advantage.

— *Emotionally-oriented*: In which we do not have the power to change the situation, but we can manage stress by changing our interpretation of the situation and the way we feel about it. If you do not have the power to change a situation, then you may be able to reduce stress by changing the way you look at it, using an emotionally-oriented approach. Emotionally-oriented approaches are often less attractive than action-oriented approaches in that the stresses can recur time and again; however, they are useful and effective in their place.

– *Acceptance-oriented*: Where something has happened over which we have no power and no emotional control, and where our focus is on surviving the stress. Sometimes, we have so little power in a situation that all we can do to survive it. This is the case, for example, when loved-ones die. In these situations, often the first stage of coping with the stress is to accept one's lack of power.

These different approaches to stress management address our definition of stress in different ways: the action-oriented techniques help us to manage the demands upon us and increase the resources we can mobilise; the emotionally oriented techniques help us to adjust our perceptions of the situation; and the acceptance-oriented techniques help us survive the situations that we genuinely cannot change.

Managing Stress with Positive Thinking

In many cases, situations do not cause all of the stress that we experience. Sometimes, our reaction to circumstances (and what we say to ourselves about them) contributes to the stress we experience.

Sometimes we are right in what we say to ourselves. Often, however, we are overly harsh and unjust in a way that we would never be with friends or co-workers. This, along with other negative thinking, can cause intense stress and unhappiness and can severely damage your self-confidence.

Negative thinking damages your performance by undermining your self-confidence. It also occupies "attentional capacity" at times when you need to focus your entire mind on what you are doing.

In becoming stressed, people must make two main judgments: First, they must feel threatened by the situation; and second, they must doubt that they can meet the threat. How stressed they feel depends on the damage they think the situation can do them, and how closely their resources meet the demands of the situation.

Perception is key to this. Being precise, situations are not stressful in their own right—rather it is our interpretation of the situation that drives the level of stress that we feel.

Quite obviously, sometimes we are right in what we say to ourselves. Some situations may actually be dangerous, and may threaten us physically, socially or in our career. Here, stress and emotion are part of the early warning system that alerts us to the threat from these situations. Often, however, we are wrong. It's easy to be overly harsh and unjust to ourselves in a way that we would never be with friends or co-workers. This, along with other negative thinking, can cause intense stress and unhappiness and can severely undermine self-confidence.

How Negative Thinking Undermines Performance?

Not only do these inappropriate negative thoughts cause a great deal of unhappiness, they also reduce our performance.One obvious part of this comes from the mental effort wasted in worrying. This is particularly important when we are focusing on a task in which we need to perform well. Here, negative and anxious thinking compete with task-related thoughts for the attentional capacity of our conscious mind, disrupting the state of flow in which we perform at our best.

Worry and anxiety often contain important information on threats that we may face. Eliminating them altogether can mean that we miss important cues from our environment, and fail to make appropriate contingency plans. However, as we say above, worry interferes with our performance.

A useful way of dealing with worry is to reschedule it: Acknowledge to yourself that you need to think the issue through, and allocate a time to do so. Keep a notebook with you and note down the worries "buzzing around" in your mind. Think the issue through at the appointed time, but in the meantime, put it out of your mind. Not only does negative thinking affect your performance, it also affects your health. People who approach the stresses of life with depression, anxiety and hostility experience significantly worse health. This is in direct contrasted with people who showed stress "hardiness". These people manage to survive intense stress with little illness. Hardiness is characterised by positive attitude to challenges, positive thinking and commitment to goals, among other things.

Thought Awareness

You are thinking negatively when you fear the future, put yourself down, criticise yourself for errors, doubt your abilities, or expect failure. Negative thinking damages confidence, harms performance and paralyses mental skills.

A major problem with this is that negative thoughts tend to flit into our consciousness, do their damage and flit back out again with their significance having barely been noticed. Since we do not challenge them, they can be completely incorrect and wrong, however this does not diminish their harmful affect.

Thought awareness is the process by which you observe your thoughts and become aware of what is going through your head. Another more general approach to thought awareness comes with logging stress in your stress diary.

One of the benefits of using the stress diary is that you log all of the unpleasant things in your life that cause you stress for one or two weeks. This will include negative thoughts and anxieties, and can also include difficult or unpleasant memories and situations that you perceive as negative.

By logging your negative thoughts for a reasonable period of time, you will quickly see patterns in your negative thinking. When you analyse your diary at the end of the period, you should be able to see the most common and the most damaging thoughts. Tackle these as a priority. Thought awareness is the first step in the process of managing negative thoughts, as you cannot manage thoughts that you are unaware of.

Rational Thinking

The next step in dealing with negative thinking is to challenge the negative thoughts that you identified. Look at every thought you wrote down and rationally challenge it. Ask yourself whether the thought is reasonable: Does it stand up to fair scrutiny? As an example, by analysing your stress diary you might identify that you have frequently had the following negative thoughts:

– *Feelings of inadequacy*: Have you trained and educated yourself as well as you reasonably should to do the job? Do you have the experience and resources you need to do it? Have you planned, prepared and rehearsed appropriately? If you have done all of these, are you setting yourself unattainably high standards for doing the job?

- *Worries about performance*: Do you have the training that a reasonable person would think is needed to do a good job? Have you planned appropriately? Do you have the information and resources you need? Have you cleared the time you need and cued up your support team appropriately? Have you prepared appropriately? If you have not, then you need to do these things quickly. If you have, then you are well positioned to give the best performance that you can.
- *Problems with issues outside your control:* Have you conducted appropriate contingency planning? Have you thought through and managed all likely risks and contingencies appropriately? If so, you will be well prepared to handle potential problems.
- *Worry about other people's reactions:* If you have put in good preparation, and you do the best you can, then that is all that you need to know. If you perform as well as you reasonably can, then fair people are likely to respond well. If people are not fair, then this is something outside your control. Often, the best thing to do is to rise above unfair comments.

If you find it difficult to look at your negative thoughts objectively, imagine that you are your best friend or a respected coach or mentor. Look at the list of negative thoughts and imagine the negative thoughts were written by someone you were giving objective advice to, and think how you would challenge these thoughts.

When you challenge negative thoughts rationally, you should be able to see quickly whether the thoughts are wrong or whether they have some substance to them. Where there is some substance, take appropriate action. In these cases, negative thinking has been an early warning system showing where you need to direct your attention.

Positive Thinking and Opportunity Seeking

Where you have used rational thinking to identify incorrect negative thinking, it can often be useful to prepare rational positive thoughts and affirmations to counter them. It can also be useful to look at the situation and see if there are any useful opportunities that are offered by it. Affirmations help you to build self-confidence. By basing your affirmations on the clear, rational assessments of facts that you made using Rational Thinking, you can use them to undo the damage that negative thinking may have done to your self-confidence. Your affirmations will be strongest if they are specific, are expressed in the present tense and have strong emotional content.

Continuing the examples above, positive affirmations might be:

— *Feelings of inadequacy*: "I am well-trained for this? I have the experience, the tools and the resources I need. I have thought through and prepared for all possible issues. I can do a superb job."

— *Worries about performance:* "I have researched and planned well for this, and I thoroughly understand the problem. I have the time, resources and help I need. I am well prepared to do an excellent job."

— *Problems issues outside your control*: "We have thought through everything that might reasonably happen and have planned how we can handle all likely contingencies. Everyone is ready to help where necessary. We are very well placed to react flexibly and effectively to unusual events."

— *Worry about other people's reaction*: "I am well-prepared and am doing the best I can. Fair people will respect this. I will rise above any unfair criticism in a mature and professional way."

If appropriate, write these affirmations down so that you can use them when you need them. As well as allowing you to structure useful affirmations, part of Positive Thinking is to look at opportunities that the situation might offer to you. In the examples above, successfully overcoming the situations causing the original negative thinking will open up opportunities. You will acquire new skills, you will be seen as someone who can handle difficult challenges, and you may open up new career opportunities.

Make sure that identifying these opportunities and focusing on them is part of your positive thinking. In the past people have advocated positive thinking almost recklessly, as if it is a solution to everything. Positive thinking should be used with common sense. First, decide rationally what goals you can realistically attain with hard work, and then use positive thinking to reinforce these. Thought awareness helps you to understand the negative thinking, unpleasant memories and misinterpretation of situations that may interfere with your performance and damage your self-confidence.

Rational thinking is the technique that helps you to challenge these negative thoughts and either learn from them or refute them as incorrect. Positive thinking is then used to create positive affirmations that you can use to counter negative thoughts. These affirmations neutralise negative thoughts and build your self-confidence. It is also used to find the opportunities that are almost always present to some degree in a difficult situation.

Managing Emotions with Positive Thinking

We are educated to believe that emotion is bad. Emotion, we are told, clouds the intellect and interferes with the objective analysis of facts. We understand that excessive emotions like intense anger have tremendous power to damage the complex social relationships on which we rely. So they do. However, this is only part of the story.

Emotions give us the benefit of a speedy, and more-often-than-not effective response to simple situations, at the cost of a sophisticated response to more complex ones. As such, negative emotions are a useful early warning signal that something may be wrong.

If instant action is required, then we may choose to act. If it is not, these negative emotions can alert us to something we need to pay attention to. We can then use more sophisticated techniques to understand the situation in appropriate detail.

Rationality of Emotion Analysis

Emotional analysis assumes that we experience different negative emotions for different, very rational reasons. It assumes that each emotion has its own underlying set of assumptions, and that we experience a particular emotion because we are making a particular set of assumptions about a situation we are experiencing.

In fact, according to the theory, there are six main automatic assumptions that can lie beneath negative emotions. These are shown in figure 2 on next page. The emotions we experience in difficult situations depend on which of these assumptions or factors apply.

Emotional analysis is a useful staring point for understanding our own strong emotions, as well as those of others. It helps us to see whether the emotions we're experiencing are alerting us to important information, or whether they are incorrectly founded or an over-reaction to the circumstances.

To use the tool, follow these steps:

— *Relax!* Once you recognised the emotion, you need to let it pass so you can think clearly and objectively.

— *Identify the assumptions you are making*: Using this as a checklist, work through it and identify the assumptions that you are making. Once you have done this, identify any other assumptions that are influencing the emotion.

— *Challenge the assumptions*: Approaching each of the assumptions one-by-one, challenge it rationally to see whether the assumption is correct or not.

Figure 2: Automatic Assumptions That Lie Behind Emotion

This list below shows some of the key automatic assumptions that we make when we experience negative emotion. Different assumptions are associated with the experience of different emotions. Only some of these will apply at any one time:

— That the situation is relevant to our goals: Goals can be formal goals or objectives that we set ourselves, or can be informal, unstated desires like wanting to drink when thirsty or eat when hungry. If the situation is not relevant to our goals or to the goals of people who are important to us, then we feel little emotion. The intensity of the emotion we feel reflects the importance of the goal.

— That the situation threatens our goals: We usually experience positive emotions in situations that support our achievement of goals and negative emotion when these are being frustrated.

— That we expect the situation to turn out badly.

— That we feel that something important to us is being threatened: We experience different emotions depending on which of the following personal factors we think are threatened:

— Our self-esteem, or the value that other people see in us

— Our ideal of how we want to see ourselves

— Our moral values

— Thoughts, ideas, philosophies and understandings of reality that we think are important

— People that we love or objects that we value

— Goals and ambitions that are important to us

— That we are responsible, or that someone else is to blame

— That we have some power to affect the situation, or that we are powerless

With each challenge, identify whether the assumptions you have made are correct or incorrect. If it helps with this, imagine as you make each challenge that you are your own best friend—do not be harsh with yourself. Be fair.

— *Take action appropriately*: Where your assumptions are incorrect, the negative emotions should change or disappear as soon as you acknowledge this. Where assumptions either have some element of truth to them or are fully correct, then you need to recognise this. Think through what you need to do to manage these situations. This may include drawing on skills explained elsewhere on this site.

Where you are sure of the foundation of the negative emotion, then you have the option to use it for good effect. For example, in the right circumstances, feeling angry can provide tremendous power and motivation. Expressing it has a shock effect that can help you achieve what you need to achieve, as long as you accept the fact that this may damage relationships.

While acting immediately on strong emotion can often leave us looking foolish, emotion should not be discounted. While strong emotion can cause us to make mistakes, it can also act as an early warning system, alerting us to threats in our environment long before we could rationally understand what's going on.

Emotional analysis helps us to understand the information content of our emotions. It allows us to challenge the underlying assumptions to see whether the are incorrect, or whether they are alerting us to important information that we need to recognise and act on.

Building Defences Against Stress

The way we live our lives can have a huge impact on the

way that we experience stress. This section shows how living a healthy lifestyle can help you reduce background stress levels. This makes you more resilient, and means that you can cope with major work stresses more effectively. This is one part of dealing with intense long-term stress. Other parts involve developing support networks to relieve stress, and adopting enjoyable pastimes to counterbalance the unpleasantness of stress.

Adopting a healthy lifestyle means that you can concentrate better and are more energetic in what you do. This is particularly important when you are in challenging or stressful situations. It is also important in building stamina.

Equally important is achieving a good work-life balance. By offsetting the unpleasant, stressful events in your life with plenty of good, enjoyable events, you make life more tolerable and reduce the risk of burnout.

Research shows the benefits of optimism and a positive frame of mind are huge: optimists enjoy better health, stronger relationships, are more productive, and experience less stress, among other things. This is because optimists tend to take more risks, and blame external circumstances if they fail, maintaining a 'try again' mindset; this makes them more likely to succeed in the future, and less upset by failure in general. Pessimists, on the other hand, tend to blame themselves when things go wrong, becoming more reluctant to try again with each negative experience in life. They begin to look at positive events in their lives as 'flukes' that have nothing to do with them, and expect the worst. In this way, optimists and pessimists both create self-fulfilling prophecies.

When you understand this, it becomes more clear how optimism and positive self-talk can impact your stress levels, as can pessimism and negative self-talk. Negative events are less stressful when you see them as 'not your fault', and less likely to recur. Similarly, positive events are even sweeter when you see them as evidence of more to come, and see yourself as the master of your own fate. Additionally, because of the difference in behaviour in optimists vs. pessimists, those who habitually practice positive thinking tend to experience more success, which can add up to a less stressful life. So how can you use this information to reduce your stress level? Fortunately, optimism can be learned. With practice, you can change your self-talk (your inner dialogue, what you say to yourself about what you're experiencing) and your explanatory style.

Take a self-test and learn whether you're an optimist or a pessimist, and to what degree. The reason that this is important is that many pessimists think they're optimists; however, optimism is defined by specific criteria. If you know where you lie on the optimism-pessimism spectrum, you'll have a better idea of what may need changing. Once you understand your current way of seeing things, you can make a conscious effort to look at things differently as you're presented with situations. Positive affirmations can also help you reprogramme yourself and your way of thinking so that positive thinking becomes more automatic and less something you need to think about consciously in each new situation.

Positive Affirmations as a Stress Management Tool

Positive affirmations are a great tool to reprogramme your unconscious mind from negative thinking to positive. The idea is to take positive statements of what you would like to see manifested, and repeat them enough so that they're part of your way of thinking and seeing the world; this operates in the same way that negative self-talk does, but in a way that benefits you. To come up with your own positive affirmations, use the following guidelines:

— *Look at your intentions*: Think about what you are trying to create in your life. This means, look at the end product, and the behaviours, attitudes and traits you would like to see yourself develop in order to get there. Would you like to feel more peace? Would you like to practice more healthy lifestyle habits? Would you like to be a more supportive friend? You might want to write in a journal and brainstorm to figure out what's important to you and get to the heart of what you want to create in your life.

— *Create statements*: Once you get an idea of what you're aiming for, try to put that idea into a few simple statements that reflect the reality of what you want to create. Phrase the statements as if they are already true, not that you would like them to be true. For example, the affirmation, "I am feeling more peaceful each day," would be better than, "I want to feel more peaceful." This is because you are programming your subconscious mind to believe the statements, and that helps manifest them into reality. You're not trying to want something, you're trying to make it so.

— *Be sure they're positive*: When making positive affirmations, be sure they're positive! This means saying what you want to see and experience, not what you don't want to see and experience. For example, instead of saying, "I don't want to feel stress," or even, "I've stopped feeling stress," use, "I'm feeling peace". Sometimes your mind doesn't register the negative, and it just hears the concept, "stress", which is what you're trying to avoid.

— *Make them realistic*: Your subconscious mind can benefit from positive affirmations that stretch and expand your perspective, but if you push things too far, your 'inner judge' steps in and negates the affirmations. Be sure that you're making your affirmations realistic, but hopeful as well, and positive affirmations will work for you.

Once you've found your affirmations, here are some fun ways to introduce positive affirmations into your life:

- *Repetition*: Probably the most popular way to harness the power of affirmations is to simply repeat them to yourself on a regular basis. Repeating them mentally several times in the morning or evening can be effective; repeating them aloud is even more effective because you hear them more clearly that way.
- *Do-it-yourself recording*: You can make a recording of yourself repeating positive affirmations and play it as you drive, get reading in the morning, or do other activities. Talk in a calm voice, maybe play your favourite soothing music in the background, and you have a recording tailor-made especially for your needs!
- *On post-its*: A fun way to use affirmations is to put them on post-its that you place around your house to give yourself positive messages throughout the day. This technique can be effective on its own, or can be used with other affirmation techniques as a reinforcer.
- *Self-hypnosis*: To really increase the effectiveness of affirmations, you can use them with self-hypnosis. This is a way to really cement them into your subconscious thinking much more quickly than repeating them in your normal conscious state.

Reduce Stress by Positive Self-talk

Patterns of negative or positive self-talk often start in childhood. Usually, the self-talk habit is one that's coloured our thinking for years, and can affect us in many ways, influencing the experience of stress to our lives. However, any time can be a good time to change it! Here are some ways you can stop yourself from using negative self-talk and use your mind to boost your productivity and self-esteem, and relieve stress.

- *Notice your patterns*: The first step toward change is to become more aware of the problem. You probably don't realise how often you say negative things in your head, or how much it affects your experience.
- *Journal writing*: Whether you carry a journal around with you and jot down negative comments when you think them, write a general summary of your thoughts at the end of the day, or just start writing about your feelings on a certain topic and later go back to analyse it for content, journaling can be an effective tool for examining your inner process.
- *Thought-stopping*: As you notice yourself saying something negative in your mind, you can stop your thought mid-stream my saying to yourself "Stop". Saying this aloud will be more powerful, and having to say it aloud will make you more aware of how many times you are stopping negative thoughts, and where.
- *Rubber-band snap*: Another therapeutic trick is to walk around with a rubber band around your wrist; as you notice negative self-talk, pull the band away from your skin and let it snap back. It'll hurt a little, and serve as a slightly negative consequence that will both make you more aware of your thoughts, and help to stop them!

Replace Negative Statements

A good way to stop a bad habit is to replace it with something better. Once you're aware of your internal dialogue, here are some ways to change it:

— *Milder wording*: Have you ever been to a hospital and noticed how the nurses talk about 'discomfort' instead of 'pain'? This is generally done because 'pain' is a much more powerful word, and discussing your 'pain' level can actually make your experience of it more intense than if you're discussing your 'discomfort' level. You can try this strategy in your daily life. In your self-talk, turning more powerful negative words to more neutral ones can actually help neutralise your experience.

— *Change negative to neutral or positive*: As you find yourself mentally complaining about something, rethink your assumptions. Are you assuming something is a negative event when it isn't, necessarily? For example, having your plans cancelled at the last minute can be seen as a negative, but what you do with your newly-freed schedule can be what you make of it. The next time you find yourself stressing about something or deciding you're not up to a challenge, stop and rethink, and see if you can come up with a neutral or positive replacement.

— *Change Self-limiting statements to questions*: Self-limiting statements like "I can't handle this!" or "This is impossible!" are particularly damaging because they increase your stress in a given situation and they stop you from searching for solutions. The next time you find yourself thinking something that limits the possibilities of a given situation, turn it into a question. Doesn't "How can I handle this?" or "How is this possible?" sound more hopeful and open up your imagination to new possibilities?

5

Building Self-confidence through Positive Thinking

The traits of self-confidence, positive thinking, and motivation are three of the pillars of self-improvement and achieving success. Weakness in any of the three traits will clip your potential level of achievement. There are more traits and abilities that come into play, of course, but these are especially important.

There is no ultimate level of self-improvement or personal confidence that can be regarded as your peak, where all self-development comes to a grinding halt. So, wherever you are now, there is further you can go. One thing that may stop you going any further is having any negative thoughts about whether it is necessary, desirable or even possible to develop yourself any further.

If you feel you need to go into new areas of development, such as a totally new career path, then there is a chance that the severity of the change will attract negative thoughts, like "why bother, I'm OK as I am." You have already built your self-confidence through success in other areas, so introducing an element of risk and failure may not be attractive. However, if you just rest on your laurels, a decline in motivation will inevitably set in, and your confidence to break new ground will wane.

It is best not to allow even a short period of negative thought to hold back your personal development. If you reach the stage where you start thinking you do not want to break new ground at all, then that is a wonderful time to go travelling. Just get on a plane and go to a country you have never been to before; a country with a totally different culture to your own.

If you can, go on your own, and go for at least three weeks. You can be sure that during that time, your mind will be cleared and inspired, and filled will the motivation for renewal. You may even surprise yourself with what action you take when you get home.

Building Self-confidence

In a way, going from a lack of self-confidence to a degree of self-confidence is easier than the previously self-confident person reaching a stumbling block and grinding to a halt. If you are lacking in self-confidence, the use of positive thinking in a particular comfort zone (such as a hobby) can help you increase your self-confidence in that area of your life.

Give yourself a short term target to achieve in your chosen arena, and visualise yourself in a respected new role within that field. Of course, action is needed as well as positive thinking, but it can play an important part. There is no need to set a high aim that is likely to disappoint you and dent your confidence. Taking a step at a time is fine, and never think that "so and so" would laugh at what your are trying to achieve. Everyone is different, and self-improvement begins and ends at a different level for all of us. One person may want to be the first person on Mars, but for others, those often lacking in confidence, something like organising an angling trip for a group of club members can be a big leap forward.

Self-confidence is about balance. At one extreme, we have people with low self-confidence. At the other end, we have people who may be over-confident. If you are under-confident, you'll avoid taking risks and stretching yourself; and you might not try at all. And if you're over-confident, you may take on too much risk, stretch yourself beyond your capabilities, and crash badly. You may also find that you're so optimistic that you don't try hard enough to truly succeed.

Getting this right is a matter of having the right amount of confidence, founded in reality and on your true ability. With the right amount of self-confidence, you will take informed risks, stretch yourself (but not beyond your abilities) and try hard.

Two main things contribute to self-confidence: self-efficacy and self-esteem. We gain a sense of self-efficacy when we see ourselves (and others similar to ourselves) mastering skills and achieving goals that matter in those skill areas. This is the confidence that, if we learn and work hard in a particular area, we'll succeed; and it's this type of confidence that leads people to accept difficult challenges, and persist in the face of setbacks.

This overlaps with the idea of self-esteem, which is a more general sense that we can cope with what's going on in our lives, and that we have a right to be happy. Partly, this comes from a feeling that the people around us approve of us, which we may or may not be able to control. However, it also comes from the sense that we are behaving virtuously, that we're competent at what we do, and that we can compete successfully when we put our minds to it.

Some people believe that self-confidence can be built with affirmations and positive thinking. At Mind Tools, we believe that there's some truth in this, but that it's just as important to build self-confidence by setting and achieving goals—thereby building competence. Without this underlying competence, you don't have self-confidence: you have shallow overconfidence, with all of the issues, upset and failure that this brings.

Believe in Yourself

Do you believe in yourself? Do you give yourself the credit you deserve? Self-esteem is an integral part of personal happiness, fulfilling relationships and achievement. This test is designed to evaluate your general level of self-esteem and determine whether you need to work on your self-image. Take the Self-esteem Test to find out your true sense of self.

Most of us live in a cocoon of fear. If it's not one thing we're afraid of it's another. What with financial stresses, employment uncertainties, relationships at work, problems with children, their schools etc., it's one merry-go-round of anxiety after another. We could be forgiven for thinking this is the only way.

Fortunately it isn't the only way. There's an infinitely better way and it's all about faith; a faith even more simplistic than a faith in God perhaps.

This is as simple as making the choice to see the virtue within you and setting out to replicate it and build on it. Virtue contributes to faith and faith brings a zest for living. Part of this is deliberately choosing to see others positive views of you. See their views of you as positive. It will help your self-esteem.

And the result, over time, is an increasing and welling up of positive confidence that will set you up for future success and so on and so on. It's a self-fulfilling prophesy. But, it will only work if you're growing genuinely in virtue i.e. being more thankful, positive, kind etc.

It's often said that if we don't believe in ourselves, who will (apart from our parents and a handful of close others)? It's strange how believing in yourself and not condemning yourself can be so powerful. Suddenly, without the chains and shackles of despair and rejection holding us down, we're able to soar like eagles—and be the way we were always meant to be. Give yourself another second chance. Believe in yourself: your abilities, your ideas, your resilience to get through your tough situation right now, and finally, your character. Life was never meant to beat us down. No matter what is against you, you can prove the greatest inspiration, even to yourself.

Developing Self-confidence through Positive Thinking

So much depends on your state of mind. Negative thoughts and feelings only bring you down and lower your confidence level. If you want to enjoy more self-confidence, utilise the power of positive thinking.

The most important step to being confident is to believe that you're worthy of being confident. This can require an entire change in your mindset until you're truly happy with the person you've become. It might not be easy, and it might not be a quick change, but it's well worth the effort.

Self-talk is one form of building confidence through positive thinking. Positive affirmations can replace negative thoughts in your mind and lead to a better self-image. You must get in the habit of praising yourself for a job well done, for trying something new or for any other behaviour that you would like to encourage.

It might seem silly at first to constantly tell yourself, "Way to go!" every time you do your job, but you need to focus on this kind of self-talk until thinking positively about yourself becomes a habit.

A more visual form of positive self-talk is to make a written list of your best qualities. Really take your time and write down every single positive thing about yourself, from the aspects of your appearance you feel proudest of, to the activities you do best. When you've finished your list, store it somewhere safe but easy to find. Whenever you start feeling down and defeated, simply pull out your list and replace the negative thoughts with your list of great qualities.

Creative visualisation is a popular technique that helps people achieve their goals. The idea of visualisation is that you repeatedly envision a desired outcome. In a way, it's a form of focused daydreaming. If you were a basketball player, you would visualise yourself sinking a free throw with perfect form. If you're working to improve your self-confidence, you would want to visualise some action that embodies confidence for you. Perhaps it would be giving a speech or being a social butterfly at a gala event. Some suggest that you should make some small movement while visualising, like touching two fingers together, in order to imprint the feeling that comes along with the vision. Then later you can bring the desired feeling to the forefront by repeating the movement. The larger idea, though, is that the visualisation is a form of practice for the outcome you would like to see.

When someone gives you a compliment, how do you react? Some people with low confidence will refuse to accept the compliment by saying something like, "Oh, I just threw this outfit together," or "It wasn't really my best work." Others accept the compliment on the surface but silently counter the sentiment in their minds. Compliments should build your confidence in your positive qualities instead of becoming a case study in how your lack confidence. Dedicate yourself to accepting compliments gracefully and without any backtalk on the part of your mind.

Are there negative people in your life? If someone seems to live only to make fun of you and put you down, you should really question whether you need that person in your life. Even if it means leaving behind a relationship or cutting ties with a family member, if a person can't respect you, you will make it without that person.

Sometimes the worst feedback we receive comes from ourselves. We say that we're stupid when we make a mistake or that we're worthless if we don't get a job. Just when you think you're feeling fine, these doubts return. In order to build confidence, you must get rid of all self-defeating thoughts. Sometimes a small punishment works as a deterrent. Perhaps you could make a commitment to putting money in a jar every time you have a negative thought about yourself or doubt your abilities. Do whatever it takes to remove these negative thoughts from your mind. It's all about balance. If you focus on positive thoughts and remove negative influences from your life, you'll be rewarded with a renewed sense of self-confidence.

Believe in Yourself and Find Success in Your Life

From the quietly confident doctor whose advice we rely on, to the charismatic confidence of an inspiring speaker, self-confident people have qualities that everyone admires.

Self-confidence is extremely important in almost every aspect of our lives, yet so many people struggle to find it. Sadly, this can be a vicious circle: People who lack self-confidence can find it difficult to become successful.

After all, most people are reluctant to back a project that's being pitched by someone who was nervous, fumbling and overly apologetic.

On the other hand, you might be persuaded by someone who speaks clearly, who holds his or her head high, who answers questions assuredly, and who readily admits when he or she does not know something.

Self-confident people inspire confidence in others: their audience, their peers, their bosses, their customers, and their friends. And gaining the confidence of others is one of the key ways in which a self-confident person finds success.

The good news is that self-confidence really can be learned and built on. And, whether you're working on your own self-confidence or building the confidence of people around you, it's well-worth the effort!

Your level of self-confidence can show in many ways: your behaviour, your body language, how you speak, what you say, and so on. Look at the following comparisons of common confident behaviour with behaviour associated with low self-confidence. Which thoughts or actions do you recognise in yourself and people around you?

Self-confident	Low Self-confidence
Doing what you believe to be right, even if others mock or criticise you for it.	Governing your behaviour based on what other people think.
Being willing to take risks and go the extra mile to achieve better things.	Staying in your comfort zone, fearing failure and so avoid taking risks.
Admitting your mistakes, and learning from them.	Working hard to cover up mistakes and hoping that you can fix the problem before anyone notices.
Waiting for others to congratulate you on your accomplishments.	Extolling your own virtues as often as possible to as many people as possible.
Accepting compliments graciously. "Thanks, I really worked hard on that prospectus. I'm pleased you recognise my efforts."	Dismissing compliments offhandedly. "Oh that prospectus was nothing really, anyone could have done it."

As you can see from these examples, low self-confidence can be self-destructive, and it often manifests itself as negativity. Self-confident people are generally more positive—they believe in themselves and their abilities, and they also believe in living life to the full.

Have you ever met a wanabe entrepreneur? You know the kind of person that talks about opening a business but never gets off the fence and does anything. Or the one that finally takes the dive, starts a business, but can never quite make it work. He spends all his time reading books but never really does anything. These people just don't believe in themselves. They don't believe they can actually become a success so they just keep doing what they've always done never moving forward. And, they always have excuses. They say:

- I'm too old to start a new career.
- I don't know enough to be in business for myself.
- I won't be able to handle it, I don't know enough
- I can't afford it.
- I will never be able to get financing.
- It will take too much time.
- Dealing with all the details will be too time-consuming.
- I don't have the spare cash.
- It is just too expensive.
- The economy is too unpredictable.

But, this is just nonsense and there are big benefits in working for yourself.

Potential Upside in Working for Yourself

- You don't have to deal with a boss.
- You set your own hours.

- You set the rules.
- You can do what you enjoy doing.
- You have job security.
- You no longer have to fight rush hour traffic.
- You will have financial freedom.
- You will feel fulfilled.
- You will have more time for your friends and family.
- The profits are yours.
- You can use your gifts and talents.
- You can save on costs.
- You will have more time.
- You can conduct business the way you want to.

So why do these wanabes throw-up these objections and obstacles? The real crux of the problem is they don't really believe in themselves. They are stuck in a cycle of negative thinking that prevents them from achieving anything. This negative thinking destroys their dreams, blinds them to opportunity, and literally stifles their success. This type of thinking can derail your success.

Steps to Building Self-confidence

So how do you build this sense of balanced self-confidence, founded on a firm appreciation of reality? The bad news is that there's no quick fix, or 5-minute solution. The good news is that building self-confidence is readily achievable, just as long as you have the focus and determination to carry things through. And what's even better is that the things you'll do to build self-confidence will also build success—after all, your confidence will come from real, solid achievement. No-one can take this away from you!

So here are our three steps to self-confidence, for which we'll use the metaphor of a journey: preparing for your journey; setting out; and accelerating towards success.

Step 1: Preparing for Your Journey

The first step involves getting yourself ready for your journey to self-confidence. You need to take stock of where you are, think about where you want to go, get yourself in the right mindset for your journey, and commit yourself to starting it and staying with it.

In preparing for your journey, do these five things:

1. *Look at what you've already achieved*: Think about your life so far, and list the ten best things you've achieved in an "Achievement Log." Perhaps you came top in an important test or exam, played a key role in an important team, produced the best sales figures in a period, did something that made a key difference in someone else's life, or delivered a project that meant a lot for your business. Put these into a smartly formatted document, which you can look at often. And then spend a few minutes each week enjoying the success you've already had!
2. *Think about your strengths*: Next, use a technique like SWOT (**S**trengths, **W**eaknesses, **O**pportunities and **T**hreats) Analysis to take a look at who and where you are. Looking at your Achievement Log, and reflecting on your recent life, think about what your friends would consider to be your strengths and weaknesses. From these, think about the opportunities and threats you face. Make sure that you enjoy a few minutes reflecting on your strengths!
3. Think about what's important to you, and where you want to go. Next, think about the things that

are really important to you, and what you want to achieve with your life. Setting and achieving goals is a key part of this, and real self-confidence comes from this. Goal setting is the process you use to set yourself targets, and measure your successful hitting of those targets. Inform your goal setting with your SWOT Analysis. Set goals that exploit your strengths, minimise your weaknesses, realise your opportunities, and control the threats you face. And having set the major goals in your life, identify the first step in each.

4. *Start managing your mind:* At this stage, you need to start managing your mind. Learn to pick up and defeat the negative self-talk which can destroy your confidence.
5. *Commit yourself to success!* The final part of preparing for the journey is to make a clear and unequivocal promise to yourself that you are absolutely committed to your journey, and that you will do all in your power to achieve it. If as you're doing it, you find doubts starting to surface, write them down and challenge them calmly and rationally. If they dissolve under scrutiny, that's great. However if they are based on genuine risks, make sure you set additional goals to manage these appropriately.

Step 2: Setting Out

This is where you start, ever so slowly, moving towards your goal. By doing the right things, and starting with small, easy wins, you'll put yourself on the path to success—and start building the self-confidence that comes with this.

1. *Build the knowledge you need to succeed: Looking* at your goals, identify the skills you'll need to achieve them. And then look at how you can acquire these

skills confidently and well. Don't just accept a sketchy, just-good-enough solution—look for a solution, a programme or a course that fully equips you to achieve what you want to achieve and, ideally, gives you a certificate or qualification you can be proud of.

2. *Focus on the basics:* When you're starting, don't try to do anything clever or elaborate. And don't reach for perfection—just enjoy doing simple things successfully and well.
3. *Set small goals, and achieve them: Starting* with the very small goals you identified in step 1, get in the habit of setting them, achieving them, and celebrating that achievement. Don't make goals particularly challenging at this stage, just get into the habit of achieving them and celebrating them. And, little by little, start piling up the successes!
4. *Keep managing your mind: Stay* on top of that positive thinking, keep celebrating and enjoying success, and keep those mental images strong. You can also use a technique like Treasure Mapping to make your visualisations even stronger!
5. *And on the other side, learn to handle failure.* Accept that mistakes happen when you're trying something new. In fact, if you get into the habit of treating mistakes as learning experiences, you can (almost) start to see them in a positive light. After all, there's a lot to be said for the saying "if it doesn't kill you, it makes you stronger!"

Set aside any negative thoughts and write down the goals you would have for yourself if your success is a guarantee. Think about the role you will play in achieving these goals. What you need to learn to get there and map your course. Layout a systematic plan and follow it.

Step 3: Accelerating Towards Success

By this stage, you'll feel your self-confidence building. You'll have completed some of the courses you started in step 2, and you'll have plenty of success to celebrate!

This is the time to start stretching yourself. Make the goals a bit bigger, and the challenges a bit tougher. Increase the size of your commitment. And extend the skills you've proven into new, but closely related arenas.As long as you keep on stretching yourself enough, but not too much, you'll find your self-confidence building apace. What's more, you'll have earned your self-confidence—because you'll have put in the hard graft necessary to be successful!

Step 4: Become a Problem-Solver

There is a solution to every problem. Never believe any problem is unsolvable. Even if the problem you are facing feels impossible at the time do not surrender to this type of thinking. Can't never did anything.

Stay away from negative thinkers, they will derail your progress by supplying you with all of the negative reasons your idea won't work. This type of thinking will derail your progress.

If you believe you can't achieve something, you probably won't. You must transform your thinking. Train yourself to believe you can achieve and you will.

Step 5: Be a Possibility Thinker

Think big! The only thing holding you back is you. If you train yourself to begin "thinking big" big things will begin to happen for you.

Challenge yourself to:

— Never label anything as impossible.

— Never let problems stop you from taking action.

- Never think that just because you don't know how to do something doesn't you can't.
- Don't let this stop you.
- Never let the fear of failure prevent you from trying.
- Never discard an idea just because you don't know anybody that has done it that way.
- Never decide something is impossible because you lack the time, money, brains, energy, talent, or skill.
- Never toss away an idea because it's not perfect.
- Never pass up something because you might not get credit.
- Never quit.

Step 6: Don't Worry about Failing

Everybody does at one time or another. It's hard. Failure can be embarrassing. But, remember that trying to do something great and failing could be one of the best things you have ever done in your life. Failure is not failure to meet your goals, but the failure to reach as high as you possibly can.

Step 7: Take Action

Just get started...Today! The biggest problem people face is inertia. Don't be a dreamer...be a doer. Don't talk big a do nothing. The world is full of dreamers, there aren't enough people who will move ahead and take the real steps towards their goals and achieve them. Stop making excuses for not starting!

Step 8: Be Enthusiastic!

Enthusiasm is the fuel for your success. It's fine to layout your goals and set aside your negative thoughts but you must ignite your enthusiasm to truly get some momentum. Don't block yours. How do you get it? Fill your mind with a positive mental attitude!

Step 9: Maintain a Positive Attitude

So if enthusiasm is the fuel and having a positive mental attitude is how you generate enthusiasm, how do you maintain the positive mental attitude?

1. Say something positive to every person you meet.
2. See something positive in every situation.
3. Force yourself to always think "It might work."
4. Become a champion of the "why not" club.
5. Act on all positive ideas.
6. Expect positive practices.
7. Be positive about things.
8. Apply positive thinking to all things you can control.
9. Do not allow negative thoughts to derail you. Refuel your positive thinking periodically.
9. Never Give-up.

Positive affirmations will give you holding-on power.

1. Do not allow yourself to feel defeated.
2. Force yourself to be tough-minded and believe you are.
3. Feel confident that there are resources you can use to support yourself.
4. You are strong...believe it.
5. Strive for victory. Turn your worst times into your best.
6. If you are truly dedicated, you will eventually win.

6

Law of Attraction and Positive Thinking

The 'Law of Attraction' is at the very corner stone of positive thinking. It is one of the reasons why positive thinking works so well. In a nutshell it can be explained as:

> "You are what you think. You attract what you think; your life is a product of your thought and belief; nothing in the world can change this fact. To alter your life the only course open to you is to alter your thinking."

It means that whatever thoughts you hold in your mind persistently, will eventually appear in your physical world.

Why is that then? Well that is a good question and there are a few theories, but it is the law and always works! So, you might as well use it whether you understand why it works or not.

Think about your own life now. What thoughts do you consistently hold in your mind and think about regularly. Do any of these ring a bell?

'I hate my job. It's too stressful and it tires me out.'

'I think I'm coming down with a cold.'

'I never have any spare money to treat my friends and family with'.

I hope it is obvious to see that thoughts like those will inevitably attract the same negative situations into your life.

For surely, if you hate your job then you will never be able to see the positive opportunities that it may offer you. If you are so firm in the belief that nothing good could ever come of your job then you are blinded to the potentially positive opportunities it may be offering you and only open to the negative possibilities. These negative thoughts hold so many people locked in to certain situations and lifestyles. People think they can never escape them.... so they never do. How can we turn this around?

Well, take a few moments just to sit and observe your thoughts. Do you create them? You may not be, but you certainly do have them. Do you decide what thoughts come in to your mind? You may not be, they are more like a constant stream that continuously flows through your mind. We seem to simply latch on to and dwell on the thoughts that we choose.

So what thoughts do you think we should dwell on. The good thoughts or the bad/negative ones. Obviously the good/positive ones. If a negative thought comes in to your mind consciously let it go and replace it with a positive one, if another comes do the same. You will be amazed at how this one simple technique can improve your life as you will no longer be allowing negative thoughts to influence you.

Consciously decide here and now that you are in charge of your thoughts, that you decide what thoughts you dwell on. Not any other influence...not your friends, colleagues at work or any one else....you are now in charge of your thoughts and your life!

And guess what...thoughts attract similar thoughts. So if you are thinking positively about something then another positive thought will usually follow. Once you start consciously deciding to think positively then it will become a habit and a pattern. You will constantly and automatically start choosing the positive thoughts. It will become a natural thing for you to do. This is how some people always seem optimistic. Once you have gotten into this positive thinking cycle then those thoughts inevitably attract the positive reality into your physical world.

You have to constantly think certain thoughts for them to manifest in your life, they don't always happen straight-away. Some do, some don't it depends what they are. You must also think the positive thought as though you are certain that it has already happened with complete faith. Through holding these positive thoughts in your mind sooner or later they will become real in your life.

LOA Principles

The Law of Attraction (LOA) does not discriminate. It always reflects back the energy you're holding. Therefore it is vital that you always 'clean up' your vibrations so that you attract exactly what you want.

The Law of Attraction is very popular for a good reason. It's a way for people to manage their lives, get things done, and get what they want. Basically, the Law of Attraction says: "like attracts like". There's a bit more to it than that, of course, and any fan of LOA can explain the more esoteric concepts.

For LOA to work for positive results, it logically follows that one has to have a positive outlook. By LOA principles, anger engenders anger; fear engenders fear. We've all seen that happen. Conversely, laughter engenders more laughter, joy engenders joy, and a positive outlook attracts others with positive outlooks. The logic is easy to follow.

Laughter and emotions can be contagious. It is hard not to laugh when in an audience that is laughing because laughter and good humour are contagious. There was a TV show called "Laughter Challenge". It was a challenge to try and get people to laugh, and the contestant had to resist the urge. Needless to say, very few contestants won!

This is why TV shows have laugh tracks. They are cues to the home audience and encourage laughter. It is hard not to cry when you see another who is in pain and suffering. Human emotions are contagious, and so are human actions. So too, when you are around successful people, you tend to think successfully and generate success for yourself.

But some attitudes are unconscious and these can get in the way of LOA. If you have low self-esteem, this is an unconscious attitude that, if not corrected, will continue to grow. You will tend to focus on the hurtful things about yourself and dismiss the complimentary ones. The same goes for you body image. If you think of yourself as an unattractive person, you won't do things to make yourself attractive—like comb your hair or brush your teeth! These problems lie in the unconscious level of thinking.

You can change your unconscious self-perceptions in many ways, through conscious affirmations (although you may automatically negate them before they can have an effect), through practice and self-awareness. You can monitor your own speech and thoughts and this can help.

More effective means directly address the unconscious mind. Hypnosis can help reverse unconscious negativity and subliminal programmes, if of good quality, can also do the same. Regardless of the method you use, shifting your mental outlook to a positive focus can help tremendously with the effectiveness of the Law of Attraction.

Millions of people were introduced to the Law of Attraction when "The Secret" came out. These people were taught that they could have what they wanted by thinking positive, being grateful and taking action. Unfortunately, because "The Secret" was not a comprehensive resource, many individuals are feeling even more frustrated and confused about how the Law of Attraction works. It's unfortunate that people believe they can have what they want by thinking positive, putting on a happy face, focusing on what they want but completely ignoring their emotions and body signals. It doesn't work this way.

Because of the Law of Attraction, the universe responds to our whole being. We are made up of energy that vibrates at a specific frequency. Everything we do, feel, think, etc. also vibrates with energy and this energy surrounds us. As we move through our lives, we are walking advertisements and the universe constantly reflects back the energy we're vibrating. It's always a perfect match. It works in the same way tuning forks work. If you strike a tuning fork, another tuning fork of the same note will also vibrate even if it's across the room.

So, when you are thinking positive but are also feeling worried, fear or doubt, the Universe picks up on all your vibrational signals and feeds back to you an experience of a similar vibration. Usually what happens is that your 'negative' emotions cancel out your positive thinking and you experience this as feeling stuck. No energy is moving. Sometimes your 'negative' emotions are stronger in frequency (they're more frequent) than your positive thinking and you attract more thoughts, emotions and experiences that help you feel more fear, worried, and doubtful. This can create spiralling-out-of-control feelings.

A girl went to college with had a problem with thinking negatively and seemed to constantly be reminding herself to think positive. So vehement were her orders it was obvious that nothing was going to change any time soon. The fact that she had to try so hard to make herself do such a laborious task as think positively meant she would be more likely to go further into negative thinking patterns. Many people have exactly this problem, thinking they have to force themselves into these new ways of thinking. Through doing this they ultimately push their real feelings and desires aside. The truth is everyone is human, and no one feels perfectly good every minute of every day. You don't want to suppress your emotions, and should instead focus on learning the art of genuinely turning a negative into a positive. As defined by the Law of Attraction, whatever you focus your energy and attention towards you will attract, even if that is something you don't want at all.

The problem most people have converting to positive thought processes is focusing on what they don't want. This doesn't mean you sit around and think "I really want to get sick", but if you think "I really don't want to get sick" it is just the same. In both scenarios you are concentrating on getting sick, and words like not and don't mean nothing to the universe. Instead of reminding yourself not to forget something, try "I will remember..."

Be very wary of hidden messages in your attempts to think positively. Stating the obvious is a good sign that you have some underlying issues of self worth, such as saying "I want a loving partner". Any partner should be loving, and it wouldn't be a thing you needed to ask the universe for if you hadn't been wounded in the past or believed you were worthy of being loved. Another example of this could be someone affirming that they "will have an accident free year": This insinuates they are deep down afraid of having one, so the underlying driving force behind the thoughts is the fear not the desire in the conscious mind.

The best way to get on top of the situation and really become a positive thinker is to be aware your feelings rather than your thoughts. When you imagine what you want, feel it and try to amplify the feelings rather than continuing thinking. Whether your feelings are relating to your current life or the life you want, stay in the positive and let them run the show for a while.

An activity to re-align you with the Law of Attraction is making a creation box: Find pictures, notes, ideas and phrases to cut out and put in the box, and make them all of things that arouse your feeling of what you want your life to be. At least weekly you can go through the box to remind yourself. Write a diary, spending time each day reporting on everything you're thankful for and then putting all the good feelings that stimulates into writing more about what you know is being attracted towards you behind the scenes.

Try seeing the art of positive thinking in a new light and instead call it positive feeling. This will further bring your goals and dreams to fruition, leaving you open to receive what you are sending out for.

Getting More Out of Law of Attraction

How do you make the Law of Attraction work every time? Get your conscious and unconscious thoughts on the same playing field. Get them playing with each other to create in harmony instead of conflict with each other.

Where our conscious and unconscious thoughts butt heads is where the Law of Attraction fails.

The greatest secret is not that we create with our thoughts but rather our thoughts create from two places in our mind: the conscious and unconscious. Many say that we only use 10% of our total mind consciously in any moment. This means 90% of our mind is being driven from our unconscious.

When we are aware of the decisions we make in each moment we are making conscious choices. When our choices are unconscious, they are decided possibly in contradiction to what we really desire. This is how unwanted habits or manifestations can control us.

A prime example is in the case of addiction. Addiction is an attachment to something unconscious that we don't want to participate with consciously. We say that we are addicted but what we are really saying is we feel out of control. We are always in control. The things we create, we genuinely want or desire on some level. Unconscious thinking might manifest as something which is contradictory to our conscious desires.. This is the inner struggle humanity has experienced for millennia.

The secret to making the Law of Attraction work every time for everyone, is to discover one's unconscious thinking in relation to what one desires to create consciously. If the unconscious thinking is in opposition to one's desires, amend the counterproductive thinking into something that will align with one's conscious desires.

Below are ten tips for boosting your positive attitude and getting more out of the Law of Attraction, and even life in general.

1. *Lighten up*: Find the appropriate beneficial humour in situations. Humour is therapeutic and has

beneficial physiological effects. It reduces stress and shifts perspective. A good sense of humour needs to be developed and practiced because humour is a learned response.

2. *Laugh, a lot*: Laughter is the physiological response to humorous situations. It consumes energy (yes, if you laugh enough, you can lose weight!) and relieves stress. If you laugh hard enough, you will even relax and get better sleep.
3. *Appreciate*: We often look at the glass as "half empty", expecting it to run out soon. Of course, that is always possible, but if we think of abundance and opportunity, the glass can fill to overflowing. When we look at the "glass", look at it from the perspective of appreciation. We all have much in life to be grateful for. Our friends, our family, our job, where we live and so on. If we count our blessings, we shift our focus to how much we really do have, and this opens the door to more. Also, it helps to realise that much we have in life is by our own doing. We are the source of our success.
4. *Expect opportunity*: We all get opportunity every day. It comes in the strangest ways. An opportunity missed can be the one we needed because often in life we must go through a series of side steps to get where we want to go. Opportunity is the pathway to success. Of course, keep a good perspective and don't chase phantoms. Someone offering an unbelievable opportunity may be just trying to take your money or trust. But you have enough common sense to know the difference between a legitimate opportunity and something that is a con.
5. *Listen to intuition*: Intuition is very difficult to describe because it is an unconscious process. Some

scientists say it does not exist because it cannot be measured. Bacteria could not be measured for centuries, yet they existed. Intuition is a gut feeling, something that says to go somewhere or do something. People report that most of the time, their intuition is right. That's because it is based on experience, and experience is knowledge. So, in the proper areas, listen to your intuition. You may be surprised at how much you know!

6. *Wonder*: We are not the centre of the Universe. The Universe is a big place filled with many things. We don't know everything, but rather think we do. Take time to wonder about the wonders that are around you. Look at the sky and the clouds. It's a free show, never stops and everybody gets a seat. The stars are the same (unless you live in a city where the lights make them difficult to see). Have you ever looked into your cat's eyes? Your cat is a sentient being with intelligence. Wonder what she's thinking? (food). Try this with your dog! (food) Those soulful eyes speak volumes of wonder that such a creature can have so much heart and devotion. Look at your pet's coat of fur. Look at the amazing intricacy in the design. If you ever tried to copy it, you'd have cause to wonder.

7. *Expect the best*: There is a popular saying: "I can't win". It can be a self-fulfilling prophecy for a number of reasons. Many companies hold raffles and contests to give away prizes. Obviously, this is for publicity. The law says, if they hold the raffle or offer to give away the prize, they have to do it. So, someone has to win. Someone always wins. But companies are often amazed at how few people enter the contest. What holds people back is that they cannot believe they can win, so they don't even try. When we expect the best, we try, because

we are looking for the best. And many times, we position ourselves in a way to facilitate that happening.

8. *Do your best*: You will not get the best if you put out less than your best. It only makes sense. A half-hearted effort says basically "I don't care." No matter what you are doing, do it all. Don't let yourself be distracted or say to yourself, "that's good enough." Do it until you know it is done well. When we do our best, we attract the best in others.
9. *Smile, say please and thank you*: We are all working in a common human society for the common good. We all deserve respect and courtesy. None of us are entitled to anything. When people do things, whether it is their job or not, a "Thank You" goes a long way to feeling good. A warm and honest smile opens doors. Whenever people talk to us or do things for us, they are sharing and giving something that is extremely valuable—their time! It does not matter that this is part of their job. Think about it. Would you rather talk to an automated answering service for customer care, or a human being? Human connection is valuable, and worthy of respect. A little goes a long way. A simple "Thank You" can make someone's day. If you make someone's day, you can be sure it will be returned by the universe.
10. *Relax*: This is a problem for many people. We often live hectic lives and don't take time out for ourselves. Take a soak in a warm bath, sit quietly in silence and listen for the voice that speaks from within. Go to a museum or art gallery and stare at a picture. Breathe deeply and calm down. Often, when we silence the noise around us, we hear the voice of inspiration.

Life is very rich and full of wonder. To get the most from the Law of Attraction, we need to use it wisely and well. It's not that hard to do, and having a positive and uplifting outlook will work wonders. Try it, and you'll see!

Law of Attraction and Positive Affirmations

To master the Law of Attraction, you have to change your beliefs. You need to make the shift from focusing on lack to focusing on abundance.

Changing your beliefs will take time and effort especially if your beliefs are deeply held. But it can be done. Once you start changing your beliefs just for a few weeks, you will start noticing some big differences in your life. The universal Law of Attraction attracts whatever you think into your life whether it is of lack or abundance, so constantly think and believe abundant thoughts. Our thoughts may include abundance about our finances, personal health, relationships and opportunities.

The easiest way to recondition your old beliefs is though repeated repetition of new beliefs. You have probably had unconscious experience with this technique. A positive example is when a sports coach uses pep talks to repeatedly tell the players that they are winners. A negative example is when a person repeatedly tells us we are no good. If we say or hear it often enough, we begin to believe it is true and the universal Law of Attraction will too.

You can use this same technique to consciously change your negative beliefs to positive beliefs, thereby changing your life. We recommend doing daily positive affirmations to really help you attract what you want into your life.

The wording of the positive affirmations should be a positively-stated sentence of about three to six words. Long sentences become cumbersome and difficult to repeat. Negatively-stated sentences using the word "not" should be used only if it is impossible to state the desired new belief in a positive way.

Sample positive affirmations:

– "I am a good person."

– "God loves me."

– "I have lots of money coming to me."

– "I love myself."

– "I am worthy."

– "I am healthy."

Feel free to experiment with different wording of the positive affirmations. Try saying the new positive affirmation out loud and feel if it resonates with your soul. Trial and error is sometimes the only way to find the best wording to express the essence of a new belief.

Law of Attraction in Everyday Life

The Law of Attraction is a universal law that applies to everyone and everything everywhere. This is a powerful law that means all action, words, thoughts, emotions, desires, goals, positive or negative, whatever focus or energy you put out into the universe, it will come back to you, for you are the creator of what you attract. Like will attract like, all forms of energy and matter vibrates at a frequency that attracts the same vibration, it is natural and unchanging.

How does the Law of Attraction work for the average person? Everybody everywhere is using the Law of Attraction on a daily basis, either consciously or unconsciously. Whenever your expectant of something, have a need or desire, the Law of Attraction is already working for you, and gaining strength to fully manifest your thoughts into reality. The Law of Attraction is working on your focus, clear ideas, and desires to attract the situations, people, places, careers, and all sorts of goals you have already designed to accomplish in life.

How to better use the Law of Attraction? Ask yourself what kind of need or desire you want to have that would impact your life in a happy way. An example might be the desire to have a better home, buying rather than renting, gaining more education or knowledge, a new car, a better job or new career, a vacation to a tropi-cal paradise or more time to do what you want, meeting new people and friends or simply having an abundances of positive encounters that benefit your life.

The Law of Attraction tools are mainly from your mind and imagination. Every thought that you have ever had has created your world today. Wayne Dyer, Ph.D., bestselling author, has written books on this very subject in *The Power of Intention: Learning to Co-create Your World Your Way* and *Real Magic: Creating Miracles in Everyday Life*. Dr. Dyer has said, "Change the way you look at things and the things you look at change". Positive thoughts and humility help shift your alignment with goals to a more harmonising, higher vibrational energy. Removing resistance, thoughts of doubt, and replacing them with "I can". Find inspiration and get connected to the field of all possibilities.

Understanding the energy source of the Law of Attraction. Having a strong intention for anything is the key. The universal Law of Attraction will respond to your concentrated thoughts and request for manifestation. What is your heart's desire? The source is always willing to give, ask and you will receive. In daily life most people are already fixed to complete a task or goal they have set for themselves. However, to facilitate motivation, meditation and prayer help in contacting the source to create a desired situation. Visualise the outcome, use positive emotions to enhance it's creation, realise that it is possible and believe it so. This self-motivation will raise your vibration level to attract from the universe that which you need and want.

Another good book is by famaous author Deepak Chopra called *The Seven Spiritual Laws of Success*. He writes about pure potentiality, Karma, and the Law of Intention. In other books he has written about the "power of coincidence" and "fulfilment of desires". Integrating Western medicine and Indian Science of Ayurveda. Dr. Chopra has blended a combination of scientific theory such as discoveries in quantum physics and New Age mysticism into an easy to understand relationship of what he calls "synchro-destiny". Dr. Chopra says, "Thoughts have a power or energy that can attracts like energy". If you are receptive and behave as if it's coming, then your manifestation will come.

Currently the concept of the Law of Attraction is more popular than ever. Books like *The Secret* by Rhonda Byrne have capitalised on the idea that positive thoughts are powerful magnets to attract health, wealth, opportunities, happiness, and anything we want. But before the dawn of the New Age movement and self-help books, Claude M. Bristol wrote a magnificent book called *The Magic of Believing*. His book drew directly on the power of attraction by stating how to become what you contemplate, how to bring success to you, how to turn your thoughts into achievements, and gain the belief that makes things happen. Mr. Bristol knew that there was some kind of powerful intuitive-psychic force that we could tap into to make the impossible possible.

The Law of Attraction isn't so much a secret but a natural universal law that anyone anywhere can use.

Throughout history great achievers have seemed to work miracles in creating wondrous things. But some may ask is it merely luck? Good action? In the right place at the right time? Talent? The Law of Attraction works in tandem with good aspects in your life, but your own mindset plays a vital part, creating a positive intention is best to assure a pleasant outcome, but follow another path of thought and the outcome could be lead to unfavourable creations. The Law of Attraction is in a constant state of flux. The science of quantum physics has proven that everything is vibrating energy, never fix, and in a state of potential. With the Law of Attraction our focus, our desire, our imagination, our thoughts, can turn this energy into reality.

7

Be Happy with Positive Thinking

Happiness is attainable for each one of us. In fact, happiness is already inside us. Then, why do seem to be so unhappy at times? Most of us have the "something is wrong" syndrome, which means that we feel there is always something wrong in some area of our lives, be it work, or with the family, or in a relationship, or with our situation in life.

We blame often our unhappiness on anything else. In a nutshell, we create the "something is wrong" syndrome so that there is always something to fix that keeps us busy, and we can also blame something or somebody else. The idea of everything being all right is scary. In other words, we have a fear of our own success and so we "invent" problems.

What would happen if everything was all right? Imagine the situation for a moment. What would you then do? How would it be if you never feared anything? Perhaps at some point you realise that you feel there's always something wrong in your life and grow tired of the feeling. Perhaps you wonder how things would be if everything felt all right; perhaps you want to accept your own greatness.

There are ways to come to feel that everything is all right. One of them is acceptance.

When you accept everything that is, and you don't judge anything, you free yourself from those "This should be this way..." thoughts. That is, you abandon negative thinking for positive thinking. When you accept it all, and specially what you now judge is bad or wrong in your life, you give yourself the chance to feel that everything is all right, and feel good. The question is: Can you be okay with it all? Even further, can you not only be okay but actually happy, perfectly fine and peaceful with it all? Then be it.

There is no good reason that you should not be happy. It doesn't matter how little you may feel that you don't deserve it, or that you think someone or something is denying it from you, you still ought to be happy. There is little point in a life where happiness isn't a legitimate objective and if we are honest with ourselves, everything that we do has some form of happiness as the ultimate aim.

Frequently, happiness comes in the form of some sort of success. This means that we have achieved an objective, met a goal and overcome challenges. Another gauge of happiness is how loved we feel. For someone else, happiness may take the form of a desired level of personal security.

Metaphysically though, we must look at happiness as being a state of mind. This tends to shed a great deal of the mystique from the idea, but there it is. And, as metaphysicians we know that we have power and control over our mental states. This isn't quite as cold and analytical as it may first appear.

The experienced metaphysician understands that his/her mental activity is limited unless partnered with their Higher Power. Without this, mental force is involved and strenuous acts of will. Although these may have their place in some belief systems, they are unnecessary and even counter-productive in metaphysics.

This is where our right to happiness comes in. As children of a benevolent Creator, we are automatic inheritors of all the good there is. Who or what is going to deny this right bestowed on us from an omnipotent being? So, we have the right to happiness. Therefore, why aren't we assuming a happy state of mind?

It seems that the major reason that we don't just accept a happy state of mind is because of conditional expectations. "I'll be happy once I get all of my bills paid." "Happiness will be mine when I find my soulmate." "I can't be happy until this is done."

Does any of this sound familiar? We just flat out won't allow ourselves to be happy until our conditions are met, and have convinced ourselves that these external conditions are going to be the cause of our happiness.

We all know of the miserable millionaire, the frustrated, though deeply in love spouse and the successful yet horribly tense executive. Their conditions were met, and perhaps temporarily, they were happy. It didn't last. That's because they were placing the responsibility for their happiness upon circumstances outside of themselves. Circumstances over which they had little or no control. Circumstances which could not keep up with the changing needs and requirements of the evolving human soul.

It leaves us to fall upon our own, inner devices. Such as deciding to be happy for no good reason at all. We can choose to be happy in our own skins, in our lives, with circumstances the way they are right here and now. We can let go of stress, fear, anger and hopelessness and choose happiness.

One of the most pathetic things we can hear from a variety of people is, "I can't be happy while _____ (fill in the blank)" When we are being honest with ourselves, we know that we can decide to assume a happy perspective on life. There may be times when we truly don't want to be happy. If so, it is wise to be truthful about it. If you have recently lost a loved one, then it's okay to not choose happiness for a while.

Perhaps this doesn't cause us adequate suffering. Maybe we "ought" to work harder, be sadder and feel more miserable before we can give ourselves permission to feel good. If we should decide that these "oughts" are not really necessary, then a remarkable thing will happen. If we should choose happiness, practice feeling happy, letting go of our daily complaints to anyone who will listen to us, berating God, and all the other myriad activities we indulge in to remind ourselves to be miserable, life will certainly begin to improve. This is a metaphysical truism. Think positively, feel happy, indulge in your creative, enthusiastic activities and you will inevitably draw more of the same into your life. Happiness is a right and a choice. Allow it a place in your life.

Definition of Happiness

The definition of happiness varies for every person. Aristotle declared, "Happiness is the meaning and the purpose of life, the whole aim and end of human existence." Happiness is commonly viewed as a fundamental goal in life. In fact, British people have rated happiness as their most important component of quality of Life. It is even more important to them than money, health, and sex! Aren't we curious to know how other people define happiness? For many, happiness is what they feel when they receive something—a material gift or some sort of favour. On the other hand, some people find it better to give than to receive. They feel so much happiness from giving and sharing what they have. This selfless act can be the most joyful experience for those people with generous hearts. "There is a wonderful mythical law of nature that the three things we crave in life—happiness, freedom, and peace of mind—are always attained by giving them to someone else," remarked by Peyton Conway March.

Happiness is also what we feel when we are satisfied with what we are doing or what we have attained or accomplished. There are people who derive happiness from their success, wealth, or power. According to Albert Schweitzer, "Success is not the key to happiness. Happiness is the key to success. If you love what you are doing, you will be successful."

What about the majority of people who are not lucky enough to achieve the dream they have long aspired for? Do they not have the right to be happy? Of course, they do! Happiness starts with appreciating and finding satisfaction from simple things that life has to offer. The affection of a spouse, children, or grandchildren, the company of friends and colleagues, and the compliments paid to us—these are some of the simple things that capture the essence of true happiness.

"Happiness is what we feel when we get what we want"—this is probably the most common notion people have about happiness. If this concept of happiness is correct, then unhappiness is what we feel when we do not get what we want.

Consider the definition above. The keyword in the definition is the word "want." The problem starts when we want something and maintain an expanding list of wants. This problem escalates when despite all efforts, only a small percentage of our wishes are fulfilled.

Unfulfilled wishes increase with time. As we grow older and fail to get what we want, we get frustrated and become unhappy. Frustration sets in when we fail to fulfil most of our desires. As we are exposed to TV, magazines, internet, and other media, we compile a list of endless and unrealistic demands. Because of this, life becomes an endless race to fulfil desires.

According to Benjamin Franklin, "There are two ways of being happy: We must either diminish our wants or augment our means — either may do — the result is the same and it is for each man to decide for himself and to do that which happens to be easier."

To break out of this cycle, we must try to manage our needs and wants. Stephen Johnson differentiates wants and needs in his book *Yes Or No: Guide To Better Decisions*. He said, "A want is a wish. A need is a necessity." We must learn to prioritise our needs over wants. Needs are things that are necessary in life, such as food, shelter, and basic necessities. Common wants are represented by latest models of cell phones, plasma TV, IPod, designer jeans, luxury cars, and the like. These are our desires, but we can continue living without these in our lives. Stephen Johnson differentiates the two concepts in a simple way, "In life, we may want a fancy house but need a loving home."

We cannot be truly happy if we keep on "wanting" or "desiring" more than what we have. Contentedness is the gateway to happiness. There is nothing wrong with having wants, just as long as these things provide a positive motivating force. It is okay as long as we find happiness and fulfilment in the process of going after our wants. Irrational wants can limit our happiness if we make these the focus of our lives; hence, these only become sources of frustration.

Happiness is a personal decision. We are in charge with our own lives. So if we truly want to be happy, let us be guided by this advice from Ken Keyes Jr., "We always have enough to be happy if we are enjoying what we do have — and not worrying about what we don't have." Real happiness comes from within us and it starts by being satisfied with what we have. It does not matter if we have little in terms of material possessions. It is finding contentment with things that we possess.

Sources of Happiness

We can find happiness right in our own home, our workplace, in school, in the company of our friends, etc. It is up to us to find the ways and means to achieve that happiness, each of us seek and long for. However, it is essential to recognise that there is no one absolute way to achieve happiness. People may have different ideas with regard to the ways of achieving happiness.

The following classifications are perceived by many people as sources of happiness:

1. Family and friends
2. Wealth
3. Position/Rank
4. Educational Achievement
5. Fame (i.e. politics, arts, sports)

Family and Friends

The very first place where happiness dwells is right in our own homes. We find happiness just by being with our family—our parents, spouse, children and grandchildren. In fact, they are our source of strength and inspiration. Having a harmonious home life gives us happiness—one that we truly cherish and treasure. True friends are also a source of happiness. The support we get from them goes a long way in helping us to get by in times of troubles. Somehow, friends make our life complete.

Wealth

A lot of people associate wealth with happiness. Almost

everywhere in the world, people are preoccupied in the acquisition of wealth. They look upon wealth as the main source of happiness. To some, wealth and happiness are synonymous.

Not that we should despise the rich and the famous or discourage others from aspiring to be so. There is nothing wrong with dreaming of becoming rich just as long as we acknowledge that wealth has limitations. Furthermore, our priorities must be clear from the very start. Clearly, we must know what should rank first in order of priorities lest we spend our days in this world meaninglessly and without hope. The pursuit of material riches should not be on top of our priority list.

How many times have we heard of people with millions of money but are willing to give it away just to have peace of mind? They live in a state of fear, that is, fear of losing their wealth through robbery or theft. They also fear for their life and the lives of those they love. These fears may even lead to sleepless nights, stress, tension, mental anguish, heart attack and death.

Understanding and accepting that happiness has nothing to do with the accumulation of wealth is perhaps the most liberating realisation we can ever come to.

Rank and Position

Can real happiness be achieved through the attainment of high rank or position in society? To many, the answer is "yes." For most people, having a high-ranking position is synonymous to power. Such persons would have the power to rule and lead. If they become "good leaders," they would be able to lead based on sound moral values and good work ethics. In return, they would earn their people's trust, obedience, support, loyalty and cooperation. Eventually, they would find happiness and satisfaction doing their job.

However, any person who is entrusted with authority and abuses it would definitely be responsible for misuse of power. His position would only be a source of misery, as he will be confronted with issues such as corruption and problems like loss of public trust, public revolt, coups d'etat, etc.

History can speak for itself. How many unwanted rulers, kings, emperors, and presidents have been overthrown? A good example is former Philippine President Ferdinand Marcos, who ruled the country for 20 long years, but his reign came to an unfortunate end. He was "thrown" out of his own country by his own people and spent years thereafter in exile.

Achievements

Can earning the highest level of education such as doctorate degrees give happiness? For people who derive happiness from learning, knowledge is power. Some successful people have attained high levels of education. However, we hear about professional people who are successful in their own fields and yet feel miserable and depressed because they feel that something is missing in their life. We hear of doctors being sued for malpractice and negligence, of judges committing suicide, and of many other sad stories that are hard to believe but are actually happening to professional people. Does education really guarantee happiness?

Fame

Fame is also associated with happiness. In sports and various careers, it is translated to victory, winning, and attaining the status of a celebrity. Are famous men and women happy? Let's take the case of sportsmen. They practically devote their whole lifetime practising to be the best at their chosen sport. However, sports can sometimes be so stressful, especially when they are carried to the extreme. Imagine the kind of pressure sportsmen have to go through to win over a game. To cope with high expectations, they take prohibited drugs to have the stamina and endurance required in their chosen field! Consider the despair, embarrassment, shame, and ridicule that they have to endure whenever they lose a game! So, let us ask ourselves—can a life exposed to such pressures and humiliation be a truly happy life?

Let's focus our attention in the field of entertainment, specifically film and stage actors, singers, dancers, etc. Is the world of entertainment a source of true happiness? It is surprising how many people still equate happiness with fun. The truth is that fun and happiness have little or nothing in common. Fun is short-lived while happiness is a more lasting and meaningful emotion.

How to Achieve Happiness?

Happiness is achievable, but it entails some effort and the right attitude. We must have the proper attitude and outlook in life to be able to focus and condition ourselves on being happy in all the challenges we face.

Between our physical and mental being, the mind has the greater influence for most of us. The body, once it is well-taken care of and sustained with basic necessities in life, can easily function. However, the mind automatically records every event, no matter how trivial. Therefore, we must be on guard with what is recorded in our mind because it can have an effect on our levels of happiness.

Marcus Aurelius cautions us, "The happiness of your life depends upon the quality of your thoughts: therefore, guard accordingly, and take care that you entertain no notions unsuitable to virtue and reasonable nature."

Inner peace greatly comes from having love and compassion in our life. The more we feel loved and the more we care for the happiness of others, the greater is our own sense of well-being. We have peace of mind if we do not have enemies. This helps remove our fears and insecurities, and gives us the strength to cope with any obstacles we may encounter.

As long as we live in this world, we are bound to encounter problems. After all, the world is not "perfect." If we just stop to demand or expect things to be perfect, then being happy may become easier. If, at times, we lose hope and become discouraged, we should remember that there is an opportunity present in the problem. We only have to search for it.

Being realistic increases our capacity to overcome troubles. With this kind of attitude, each new obstacle can be seen as another opportunity for improvement. Let us cite one example: Two men have just lost their jobs. Instead of feeling sorry for himself, Mr. A., decides to take it as an opportunity to explore new things and find a better job. Mr. B., also facing the same circumstances, decides to jump off a twenty-storey building to end it all!

Here we see how two persons react differently under the same situation. It only means that only we can decide on how to react to every event that happens in our lives. Being happy is not always easy. It can be one of the greatest challenges we have to face in life, since it requires all the determination, persistence, and self-discipline that we can gather. It also takes a lot of maturity to be able to take responsibility in choosing to focus on what we have, rather than on what we do not have. As long as we impractically yearn for much more than what we have, in terms of wealth or luxury, we will be unhappy. This is different from having a passion or desire and being motivated to reach it, wherein we are excited or thrilled in our journey to attain it.

For most of us, enough is a little more than what we have. We often get envious of what our richer neighbours have. Sometimes, we fail to realise how lucky we are, compared to those who are less fortunate. An increase in wealth does not guarantee happiness. It is obvious that happiness does not come from material things that we focus on everyday. To discover the secret to achieving contentment and happiness is to know how to enjoy what you have and manage the desire for things currently beyond our reach.

Boost Your Happiness with Positive Thinking

You can boost your happiness by focusing on positive things and reducing your negative thinking. You'll practice doing that this week by following a negative thought with a positive one. This practice will help to retrain your habitual thought patterns to bring more positive thoughts to your life.

The ratio of positive to negative thoughts is a major factor in overall happiness. Your brain is constantly monitoring the emotional tone of your thoughts—too many negative thoughts and your brain responds by creating stress and sadness in your body. When you add more positive thoughts, your brain will create relaxation and happiness. By training yourself to follow (or negate) negative thoughts with positive ones, you'll improve your positive/negative thought ratio and be happier.

After you're aware of your negative thoughts and feelings and work to counteract them for a few days, they will gradually begin to lessen. You'll be able to concentrate more on what you want to do without experiencing distracting emotions and stress. This will make you more productive and energetic. Best of all, it will make you happier.Keep practicing the smiling technique from last week. It will help reinforce and strengthen the effects of this skill.

Achieving Happiness in Unfortunate Situations

Certain situations present big challenges for us. These are situations when most people have difficulty in finding joy and happiness. These situations include loss and grief, trials in life, troubled relationships, solitary life, and old age. Can we really find happiness in these?

Happiness in Times of Loss or Grief

Indeed, one of the most painful things in life is losing a loved one. Most, if not all, would rather avoid going through it. Losing a job or a relationship cannot be more painful than losing someone we love. The loss of a loved one is indeed a source of unhappiness and can result to a range of emotions that include sadness, grief, and uncertainty. As these feelings sink in, harsh realities would confront the survivors. Death in the family can be emotionally draining. It can also put a strain on savings and finances especially if the deceased had a protracted bout with a fatal disease. Piled up hospital bills, doctors' fees, and skyrocketing cost of medication and funeral expenses could easily upset a family's financial standing.

Death in the family also entails major adjustments and adaptation in roles and in daily activities. It is a life-changing event that requires the bereaved to pick up the pieces and go on with life. Dealing with loss and grief could be very trying indeed. To overcome grief, we have to find ways that will best work for us.

1. *Realise that time heals all wounds*. It may take some time before the pain goes away; but eventually, it will subside.
2. *Express and share grief.* Talking to someone, a friend or a loved one, is one of the proven strategies for coping up with grief. In releasing our emotions, we are actually unloading the excessive burden we may be harbouring inside us.

3. *Accept the fact that death is inevitable.* However painful it is, we must face the truth that everyone must die some day. No one is exempt from it.
4. *Move on.* Grieving is a natural reaction to death of a loved one. In fact, the grieving process is necessary in order to release the pain and hurt we feel inside. However, we cannot just focus on our loss and shut everything out. We must learn to count our blessings and try to move on with our lives.
5. *Gain a new perspective.* From a human point of view, a person may feel guilty from that loss. He may think that he could have done more to prevent the loss. On the other hand, if we will just look at things from a divine perspective, we would realise that everything happens for a reason. Death may be a respite for a relative who has suffered long enough from an incurable disease. Death finally puts an end to unbearable pain and sufferings brought about by an illness.
6. *Consider seeking professional help.* Doctors may prescribe some form of antidepressants, especially if the state of grief is prolonged and unrelenting.

Happiness during Trials

Life is full of trials. For every trial that we go through in life, our faith, patience, and strength are tested. We may encounter some hardships, but we can always choose to fight challenges and face it with hope and conviction.

Trials are part of life. We simply cannot evade them; but if handled well, they can strengthen us, build our character, and strengthen our faith. Therefore, we should try to face them as courageously as we can. We should never give up or lose hope when nothing seems right. As with all other barriers to happiness, we must do everything possible to overcome trials that come our way.

Happiness in Amidst of Troubled Relationships

Relationship gone sour is another cause of unhappiness. Problematic marital and family relationships impinge on our ability to enjoy almost anything. Individual differences and lack of communication and quality time together are some of the identified causes of relationship break-ups. However, the following are ways to patch things up and improve relationships:

1. *Find a place where both parties can be alone and have a conversation.* This way, both parties can discuss things without interruptions and distractions like TV or radio. Agree that the conversation will focus only on the issues concerned.
2. *Refrain from verbal outbursts.* Refrain from yelling or the civil conversation will lead to a shouting bout! Do not interrupt while the other person is talking. We must allow the other person to finish his or her piece before we give ours.
3. *Avoid labelling or calling names.* Personal attacks will only worsen the situation. We must be extremely careful with what we say. Do away with words that may hurt or put the other party down.
4. *Discuss the problem rationally.* We must learn to negotiate and compromise on things we want from one another.
5. *Focus on rebuilding the relationship.* This is especially true for married couples. Spend quality time together. Find time to do something together—like activities or sports.
6. *We must let them know what we want or expect from them.* In doing this, we must not demand our partner to change in order to meet our expectations. Focus on the other party's positive qualities rather than the negatives.

7. *Give and graciously receive adequate support.* This will help the relationship to survive and flourish.
8. *Consider all possible options before deciding on one solution to the problem.* However, never consider separation or divorce as an option.

Learn to forgive and forget. Give the relationship another chance.

Happiness in a Solitary Life

Leading a solo life can be very lonely. It is important to have someone to talk and relate to. It is always nice to have someone lending an ear to what we have to say. Unhappiness stems from not being able to share happenings in our life with others. In this case, we should keep in close touch with relatives and a small circle of friends and be prepared to give and receive love and support.

Robert Louis Stevenson advises people living alone to have many interests. This will enable us to meet new people. Furthermore, he tells people to keep busy at something, "A busy person never has time to be unhappy."

In addition, the following tips can be considered:

1. *Flex the mental muscles.* To avoid stagnation, we can attend seminars on different subjects.
2. *Travel and seek new places.* We should go out and travel to places we have never seen before. If we can afford it, we can take regular holidays in different countries and savour different cultures. One fascinating country is Bhutan. This remote Himalayan kingdom earned the distinction of being "the only country in the world which puts happiness at the heart of government policy."
3. *Be adventurous.* We can do something we have never done before, like visiting a particular art

gallery or going to a ballet or pick new books. This will make our lives interesting and exciting.

4. *Invest in relationships.* Surrounding ourselves with supportive family and friends is one step leading to happiness. Understanding this encourages us to invest our time and energy in developing, enhancing, and maintaining close friendships and many acquaintances.

Happiness in Old Age

Some people lose their will to live when they start to see and feel the first signs of aging. They think they can no longer do the things they used to do when they were younger. Like all others, this negative thought is all in the mind. To make our mature years happy and productive, consider the following tips:

1. *Maintain a positive attitude.* An elderly person who maintains a positive attitude in life is more likely to cope with any physical difficulty or limitation related to aging. Be productive members of society. Have a purpose in life—a reason to live! Stop entertaining negative thoughts such as "I'm already old, I only have a few years to live"; "I'm old that's why I'm sickly", etc.

2. *Stay active and eat well.* Instead of sitting around waiting to die, make the remaining years fruitful and rewarding by developing a hobby, travelling, or simply doing worthwhile activities. It has been estimated that 90% of age-related diseases are in fact, largely attributable to poor nutrition and lack of exercise. Therefore, maintaining a healthy body through exercise and nutrition is the best way to always be "alive and kicking".

3. *Be watchful and cautious.* There is a saying that "An ounce of prevention is worth a pound or cure". This

is especially true when it comes to maintaining a healthy lifestyle. Elderly people should always be extra cautious for disorders related to aging such as depression, anxiety, senility, drug dependency, immobility, etc. When the first symptoms appear, address these before these get worse. Seek medical help so the doctor can prescribe the proper medication.

4. *Nothing beats preparation.* Roger Darlington states, "It is never too young to start planning our retirement. Regularly increase your mortgage repayments and pension contributions—this is a sensible use of the money you don't need for current expenditure and it will increase your longer-term and comfortable lifestyle options."

Indeed the situations enumerated above are regrettable. Should these provide us the perfect excuse to wallow in unhappiness? When confronted with such situations, keep in mind that we can still make the best of our circumstances. Robert Louis Stevenson said, "No one has everything, and everyone has something of sorrow intermingled with gladness of life. The trick is to make the laughter outweigh the tears."

Keys to Live a Happier Life

We have already learned that happiness goes beyond material things. This is echoed by William Barclay when he said, "Joy has nothing to do with material things, or with man's outward circumstance. A man living in the lap of luxury can be wretched and a man in depths of poverty can overflow with joy."

Happiness can be induced by many ways and means. Some result to short-term happiness, while others have long lasting results. In a busy world where everyone and everything seem to be moving in a fast pace, we can do ourselves a great favour by taking time off for self-reflection. Meditation is a powerful tool for inducing happiness. Through meditation, we can reach a level of mental clarity. Making meditation a regular part of our lives will lead us to new and exciting possibilities for our inner peace. This will enhance happiness as a result.

In order to be happy, we should concentrate on happy thoughts. Happy thoughts are special and memorable moments in our lives. These thoughts are available to us every single day. All we have to do is to recall these blissful moments. For example, we recall the times when we were in love, when we were overwhelmed with feelings of joy. It was during those moments that we were in love with life itself.

The problem with some people is that they tend to remember the negative things longer than the positive things that happened in their lives. They usually remember the compliments they received only for a few minutes and dwell on the insults they received for years! By so doing, they become garbage collectors who carry trash thrown long time ago. As a result, they suffer the consequences since they allow their mind to be occupied by bad experiences.

Remember, we are in control of our own mind and heart. We can choose to make happiness and joy the centre of our world. These are always within us. We can always tap into moments of joy and absorb these into our present moment.

No one in his or her right mind would choose to be unhappy. If we take full responsibility for our emotional response to all events in our life, there is nobody else to blame if we are not happy! The choice is ours alone. Happiness does not depend solely on the things that come into our life, but on how we react when those things happen.

Mildred Barthel states, "Happiness is a conscious choice, not an automatic response." We can always create and build our lives around joy and happiness.

How do we go about enhancing happiness and pursuing it whole year round? We know happiness is far more than just money, fame, or power. Many people have all three but are not completely happy. What are the secrets to long-lasting happiness?

According to Margaret Bonnano, "It is only possible to live happily ever after on a day-to-day basis." If we want happiness all year round, we have to start small by having a good day every day. Small efforts build up through the day. Norman Lear teaches us, "Life is made up of small pleasures. Happiness is made up of those tiny successes. The big ones come too infrequently. And if you don't collect all these tiny successes, the big ones don't really mean anything."

How do we accomplish this? There is a simple way that we can do at the start of our day. As we wake up each morning, we decide that our day will be as happy and stress-free as we hope it would be. The first thing to do is we ask ourselves, "What do I wish for today?" Feel the desire and then remember that whatever we wished for, we will surely get it as long as we try to make it happen. Ask from God/the Universe and we can never go wrong.

We seek happiness practically every day of our lives. Despite our efforts, many of us are not happy. Everyone's life is spent in pursuit of happiness. We become too busy and preoccupied, working to ensure that our future will be secured and happy. We tend to let days, months, and even years slip by without realising that "time is gold."

It is fine to work towards future goals, but do not forget that today will never come again. We only have twenty-four hours to enjoy it so we should take every opportunity to make ourselves happy, including the people we love.

How many minutes, hours, and days have we spent being happy from within? Those are the only moments we have really lived life. Perhaps, we were just kids then when we were completely happy and worry-free, or there were few moments when we were doing something we really love and enjoy.

Live in the Present Moment

"Happiness is a journey, not a destination; happiness is to be found along the way not at the end of the road, for then the journey is over and it's too late. The time for happiness is today not tomorrow," said Paul Dunn. Many of us spend much of our lives worrying about the future and a number of things—all at the same time. We allow past problems and future concerns to dominate our present moments, so much so that we end up feeling frustrated and depressed.

When our attention is in the present moment, we push away fear from our minds. Fear is the concern over events that might happen in the future. To overcome fear, the best strategy is to learn to bring our attention back to the present. We must practice keeping our attention on the present. Surely, our efforts will pay off in the end.

Live in the moment with joy, alertness, awareness, and compassion. The thought of being like a child again is exhilarating. This stems from being free and feeling at home with everybody. This emanates from living without barriers, judgments, and worries about what others might think.

Whatever they think, it is their opinion and is not permanenet. Keep in mind those opinions change all the time. Worrying takes a lot of toll on the body and mind. It is like a wind that takes us away from ourselves.

Worrying leads only to fear and can paralyse us from taking appropriate actions. We free our minds from worries by relaxing and doing some breathing exercises. A simple breathing exercise consists of inhaling deep breath through the nose and exhaling through the mouth. Do this three times consecutively. This will help put our minds at ease and has a calming effect. By doing this on regular intervals, we will then find so much peace and harmony around. Remember that the art of living lies in living at the present moment.

Fill with Love

Love is the foundation of human existence. We need to feel loved to be happy. It is crucial that we have at least one person whose company we enjoy to share our life with. This does not have to be a romantic relationship. A family member or a friend can fill this need.

Many of us aspire to live a life filled with love. For this to happen, the effort must start from us. Rather than waiting for other people to provide the love we desire, we must be the source of love ourselves. Our attitude, choices, acts of kindness, and willingness to be the first to reach out, will take us towards this goal. By converting our hearts to fountains of love, we are taking an important step in getting the love we desire. We will also discover that the more love we give, the more we will receive.

Everybody wants to love and be loved by others. If we want to have a happy and harmonious home life, we have to get along well with the people around us and earn their trust and respect. We can get involved in social and community affairs, and this can result in having happy interactions with other people. Making a difference in the lives of people, who are virtual strangers, can give us a deep feeling of happiness. We can do this by volunteering our time, effort, and money in various causes.

Love makes the world go round. The need for love lies at the very core of our existence as human beings. Love brings us the greatest happiness because we treasure it over and above everything else. We cannot and will not survive if we are left alone by ourselves.

Realise the Power of Positive Thoughts

It is very important that we realise the relationship between our thoughts and the way we feel. Did you know that we are constantly thinking? Take breathing for example. Unless we feel that we are running out of breath, we simply forget that we breathe automatically.

Thinking works the same way. Since we are always doing it, it is easy to forget that it is happening. To think is to create. Everything starts in the mind. What precedes the feeling of anger? Angry thoughts precede anger. Have you tried getting angry without having angry thoughts first? Try feeling sad without sad thoughts. It is impossible!

In order to experience a feeling, we must first have the thought that induces that feeling. Happiness cannot exist alone. It is the result of positive thinking. This simple awareness is the first step in putting us back on the path towards happiness.

We should never underestimate the power of a simple thought. It may seem so innocent and fleeting; yet, it has energy that can cause great impact on our mind, body, and emotions.

Let us think of a lemon. Imagine cutting it in half and smelling it. Now, imagine squeezing the juice from the lemon into your mouth and feel those pulp bits bursting inside your mouth. Most of us will surely feel our salivary glands responding to the thought of lemon.

Indeed, what we are thinking can greatly influence our emotions. Think of someone you love. What do you feel? Now think of someone you hate. What do you feel? We do not have to change our emotions consciously—just change our thoughts and our emotions will immediately follow.

Notice that when we focus our mind on positive things, we feel better, whereas when our thoughts are focused on the negative, we feel bad. Positive thoughts yield positive results. These thoughts make us more loving and caring, resulting to good health, wealth, and happiness. On the other hand, negative thoughts produce negative results. These types of thoughts result to indifference, disease, fear and misery, etc. In other words, our thoughts create our reality.

Productive Activity

People feel a sense of achievement just by knowing that they can still contribute their skills and are needed by the people around them. Doing productive work or activity boosts our self-confidence and self-esteem, which eventually leads to happiness.

Work does not seem a burden when we are having fun. Working, while having fun, is most rewarding. If we love what we do, it will not feel like we are working at all. If we are not satisfied with our job, we look for more interesting and challenging work. Of course, we all want to make a good living but more than that, we truly have to enjoy our occupation or profession to be able to do it on a sustained basis.

Positive Attitude

A person with a negative attitude in life can never be happy. A positive attitude is needed to ensure long and lasting happiness. A perfectionist would likely be upset when the world is not the way he wants it, but a person with a positive attitude would be tolerant and understanding with all kinds of people, events, and circumstances. It has already been proven that having a positive attitude will not only lead to improvements, but it also guarantees a healthier and longer life. Two American universities have studied 1,500 people for seven long years. All 1,500 were in good health when the study started. Researchers observed how they aged by measuring their weight loss, walking speed, exhaustion, and the strength of their grip. They discovered that people who maintained a positive attitude were significantly less likely to show signs of aging. They were less likely to become weak and more likely to be stronger and healthier than those who have negative attitude. They also found out that beliefs have a direct impact on health—because our beliefs actually alter our body's chemical balance.

So let us start thinking positively! Change the way we think and believe. We alone have the power to improve our lives by having a positive attitude and a positive belief system. We can start by believing in the power of God/the Universe and prayer. Trust that whatever we ask of Him, He will surely give it to us knowing that we have pure intentions. Researchers have also proven that a positive thinker is more likely to succeed in life because positive thinking boosts self-esteem and self-confidence.

Never Set Conditions for Happiness

According to Arthur Rubinstein, "Most people ask for happiness on condition. Happiness can only be felt if you don't set any condition." Do you know someone who constantly says, "If I find the right partner, I will be happy"? Advise them to talk to newly married couples and ask them if they are happy. One of the possible things they may hear is this: "If we have a child, we will feel complete and happy."

Ask those who already have children if they are happy. They would say that unless their children have grown up, finished their studies, and can stand on their own, they simply could not relax and feel happy. Ask those who have accomplished their mission as parents if they are happy. They long for the days when they were younger!

Do you know of people who say any of the following phrases?

— I will be happy when.....

— I am unhappy because......

— If only I have.... then I will be happy

— How can I be happy when....

— Happiness for me is when ....

Sadly, these people will have difficulty in attaining true and lasting happiness for they place conditions on their happiness. They want guarantees for happiness but are unwilling to act first. For this reason, they set conditions on their happiness that can be translated into this: "We are not happy now and we won't be happy at least until our conditions are met."

On the other hand, we also hear the following phrases from unhappy people:

— You disappoint me!

— You make me unhappy!

— If it wasn't for him I'd be happy.

— She is the source of my loneliness.

— How can I be happy after what he did to me?

These people remain in constant state of unhappiness because of a single reason: the tendency to point the blame on others. Unhappiness begins in the mind. We are in charge of our mind and of what we think. If this is the case, how can we blame others for making us unhappy? We choose our thoughts and feelings. We choose to be happy or not. In this case, we made the wrong choice.

Dislodge Negative Thoughts

Like cancer, negative thinking can kill! It can kill and destroy our whole future. Negative thoughts affect the mind, body, and emotions.

Just to recap, our thoughts produce our feelings. We get angry by having angry thoughts. It is impossible to feel sad without sad thoughts. Unhappiness does not and cannot exist on its own. Unhappiness is the feeling that accompanies negative thinking.

So how do we overcome negative thoughts? Stop thinking about them! Our negative feelings are results of our own negative thinking. Apart from refraining to think about negative thoughts, we can turn negative thoughts into positive ones.

How do we go about dislodging thoughts of unhappiness?

1. *Be aware.* We have to catch ourselves when we are about to indulge in negative thinking. In the first few days, we have to be very vigilant.
2. *The moment we feel the onset of an unpleasant emotion, we have to identify it as precisely as possible.* Is it hatred? Hurt? Fear? Anxiety? Discontent? This is a very critical component of the process as related to the next step.
3. *Search for the exact opposite of the negative emotion.* Think of its antonym. For example, the moment we catch ourselves feeling "lazy," we would call to mind an opposite adjective like "energetic." We would then say to ourselves, "I feel energetic."

If we view ourselves as "pessimistic", we say "I am hopeful." If we feel we are "incompetent', we say "I feel ingenious." What do we say if we see ourselves as "unmindful"? We say, "I am grateful."

Can we use the same strategy even if we do not feel any unpleasant feelings? Of course! We are encouraged to think and say to ourselves statements like "I feel fabulous" to reinforce our mood, or statements like "I feel strong" or "I feel friendly" in order to enhance our character. Other people have introduced variations to the said technique. Others say it aloud in front of the mirror every morning for ten minutes for twenty-one days. Saying it aloud increases its effectiveness as it represents emotional involvement. This is no different from expressing positive affirmations and doing self-talk. Others find it more effective by writing the statements on paper, as they become more "physically" involved.

Boomerang Principle of Happiness

The Boomerang Principle is based on the idea that a smile is always returned. Try doing this activity on a busy location. Establish eye contact with a person (choose non-aggressive persons!) and just flash those pearly whites. Most of the time, that person will smile back. There is wisdom in smiling. Smiling always stirs pleasant feelings. A simple smile effectively communicates our happiness to others. It also makes people to feel good about themselves and encourages them spread the pleasant feeling. Rabbi Nachman puts it this way, "Always wear a smile. The gift of life will then be yours to give."

Achieve Financial Independence

Basic income should meet the family's basic needs. This frees us from worries about basic needs and concentrates on pursuing what we love best. Basic needs vary from one family to another. What is implied here is income to provide for reasonable food, clothing, and shelter. What is reasonable and enough depends upon the family's needs. Being financially independent means being free from money worries. Likewise, it means not having to depend on others for livelihood. It is having enough money in the bank that can support our lifestyle once we decide to retire. The act of saving and efficient management of our investments throughout our working lives will eventually bring us to happiness. For some this is the point where they will never have to work again.

Go for Inner Peace

Peace of mind is essential for one to be happy. Inner peace is reflected in the face. We become more relaxed and stress-free. Having peace of mind also means better over-all health. When we are healthy—physically, mentally, and emotionally—our relationships with the people around us tend to get better. The greater our over-all peace of mind, the more likely we will achieve happiness.

Achieve Good Health

Health is wealth. Good health is a very important factor in achieving happiness. It allows us to make life more enjoyable. On the other hand, an illness not only drains the pocket, but it also destroys our zest in life. Therefore, the body must be treated well, pampered with love, and given the needed nourishment. We take good care of it by taking preventive measures. We can opt to engage in a healthy lifestyle by eating the right foods and doing regular exercise.

Trio of Happiness

Current trends show that more and more people engage in writing "Thank You Journals". Psychologists explain that daily expressions of gratitude have a lot to do with life satisfaction. "Talking and writing about what they're grateful for amplifies adults' happiness," they report.

Keep a diary, which is a wonderful way to reminisce good times. More importantly, it is a reminder that bad times don't last. Some people include photos in their diaries and journals. Looking at happy times and old friends induces the feeling of joy.

Another trait strongly associated with happiness is forgiveness. It is associated with feelings of inner peace. University of Michigan psychologist Christopher Peterson says, "It's the queen of all virtues, and probably the hardest to come by."

Altruistic acts boost happiness in the giver. This need not come in the form of donating money. It can be as simple as volunteering our time, service, and skills for notable causes. There is joy in giving.

If we want a happy life, we should study the lifestyle, attitude, or behaviour of happy people. Observe and understand what they do, then adopt their behaviour and attitudes. Here are some things habitually happy people do:

1. They always choose to be happy. They never give themselves the option to be unhappy. They have a terrific sense of humour.
2. They try to have a good time as often as possible. They go out, and have fun with friends and loved ones.
3. They choose only the attitudes that can help them succeed and be happy. Happy people have complete control over how they want to think and feel.
4. They follow the Golden Rule, "Do not do unto others what you do not want others to do unto

you." Habitually happy people are kind, caring, and compassionate. They do not speak ill against anybody. Having a clean conscience gives them long-lasting happiness.

5. They have fighting spirit. They do not let other people control their emotions and actions. Likewise, they stay away from those who try to drag their spirits down.
6. They never dwell on the past. Contrary to what others say, happy people are realistic as they accept the fact that life is not a bed of roses. Storms of life come and go; it is part of life. They never let bad and sad experiences ruin the rest of their lives. Remember that there is always a rainbow after a storm. They always move on with life and let time heal the wound. Joyful people face the future optimistically.

Being habitually happy takes a lot of practice and effort. We have to develop certain attitudes and behaviour to be able to achieve happiness all year round. We can do this gradually by becoming more disciplined and determined in choosing to make happiness part of our lifestyle.

Enjoy Your Life

Understandably, life can be boring sometimes. Our daily routine becomes very monotonous when we do the same old things every day. We can try to add new things into our lives, among these are the following:

1. Visit new and exciting places. Doing this keeps life very exciting.
2. Try to do something new—something never done before, like taking up a new sport or hobby.
3. Do enjoyable things. These will not only give us pleasure and excitement, but also keep our worries

away. A worry-free life means a longer, healthier, and happier life.

4. For a change, we should try out the things we dread to do. Overcoming our fears is the only way to free ourselves from limitations. By doing this, we will gain more confidence and feel greater happiness.

Happiness is learning to draw satisfaction and contentment from whatever available resources we may have. Consider these as our blessings! However, there are people who find it difficult to be contented. In most cases, the problem lies in their nature. These are the kind of people who always think negatively and take life so seriously. Rather than being content and grateful for what they have, they are focused on what is wrong with their lives and on their obsessive need to fix problems.

The very act of focusing on imperfection and negatives pulls us away from our goal to be happy. The solution here is to catch ourselves when we fall into the habit of insisting that things should be other than what they are. Conditioning the mind to reject negative thoughts, which later turn to negative emotions, requires a lot of determination. There should be an inner desire to remove such thoughts. As we begin to eliminate the negative thoughts in all areas of our life, we will begin to discover the positive side of life itself.

We appreciate our blessings by:

— Maintaining an optimistic attitude
— Living our dreams
— Understanding that failure is not the end of the world
— Welcoming new challenges and experiences
— Working on important goals

- Thinking about our past successes and not failures
- Trying to find goodness in everything and every person

A long, healthy and happy life is what we all aspire for. However, there is no single absolute way to arrive at this kind of life. We can consider tips and guidelines to hasten our journey and to make it smoother. Put these into action and be pleasantly surprised by their inherent power of life transformation!

Happiness with Positive Thinking Tips

Being a negative thinker is very unhealthy as it lowers your self-esteem and bad for your morale. It drains your energy rapidly and causes you to lose focus. To stop being a negative thinker, you have to change your thoughts pattern.

1. The first tip to being positive is to look after your body and mind. To ensure that you are in a good shape, eat well, exercise regularly, sleep well and spend time with your family. A relaxed and healthy body is a natural attractant for positive energy.
2. Reject and delete any negative thoughts that flashed through your mind. Researchers found out that an average person has about 60, 000 thoughts being flashed through his mind on a single day. Why should anyone cling onto a negative thought? Make a conscious decision, and do your best to rid of any negative thoughts.
3. Hug your loved ones. By hugging, it increases your self-esteem. It makes you feel comfortable and loved. Move past a cold and sturdy handshake, and hug someone you really love and care for.
4. Make sure that you surround yourself with happy, cheerful people. Avoid friends who think poorly of

themselves. This way your mind will always pick up positive vibes.

5. On a piece of paper, write down all the things that you are happy and grateful for. They can be your friends, your colleagues and your family. After you are done with the writing, paste the list somewhere it is conspicuous so that you can see it everyday. This will remind you of all the things you are grateful for and not take the things you have now for granted. Most importantly, it keeps you happy too.
6. Get out of the habit of fixing labels to people and situations. Don't say "I always knew it" "I always said so" "She never cared for me" "You have always used me", etc. Such negative thoughts put you on a negative footing. They also lower your self-esteem.
7. Do not ever be afraid to speak up. You will never gain confidence if you do. You do not need to bother what others might view you as if you speak up as you are living your own life, not others. Opportunities may slip away if you remain silent.
8. Don't think of the negative stuff when something happened. When your boss asks for you, don't think of him reprimanding you or giving you a sack. Life is unpredictable; he may want to give you a raise in salary for your excellent performance.
9. Extend a helping hand to those in need. You can read a story to your neighbour's mother who is crippled and can't move; or you may go out and trim the garden of an orphanage on a weekend you are free. You will find that these small gestures have a wonderful way of generating positive energy. They make you feel warm, energetic and wanted.

10. There may be times when you find it impossible to get rid of negative thoughts. In such situations you should go out of your house for a walk or a jog. You can even go to the gym and do some light exercises. Such activity takes your mind off the negative thoughts.

The mind is the moulder of our personal and communal world. Every event we perceive through our senses is analysed, evaluated and registered in the mind as pleasant, unpleasant or neutral. Our belief systems seek to determine whether each perceived input is something, which will "protect" or "endanger" our security, self-worth and/or freedom.

When life's events are interpreted by our programmed mind as threatening, fearful or unpleasant, we experience a state of anxiety and tension. When anxiety and nervous tension become a chronic situation, then the body and mind are gradually worn down into a state of weakness and ill health. A psychosomatic illness is created.

The energy flow, concentration and clarity of the mind are disturbed. Organs begin to malfunction. Negative emotional states such as depression, bitterness, fear, anger, hate, envy, jealousy and resentment dominate the mind. Our relationships begin to deteriorate and a feeling of alienation can set it. It is time for "Attitude Therapy."

In "Attitude Therapy" we transform attitudes, beliefs or perceptions, which prevent us from experiencing health, happiness and harmony. Negative, life-destroying attitudes are replaced by positive life-building ones. Let us consider some of these beneficial attitudes.

We create our health, illness, happiness, unhappiness, unity, alienation, joys and problems through our ways of thinking, behaving, eating, sleeping, living and interacting. When we eat poorly, do not exercise, sleep too little or too much, do not breathe properly and waste our mental and emotional energy on so many superficial pursuits, we will naturally lose our health and peace of mind.

We create our reality in four basic ways.

(a) Our choices, thoughts, actions and reactions of the past create corresponding results in our present life and psychosomatic state. (If in fact there is such a reality as reincarnation, then our past will also include all our choices of past lives.) Thus, a considerable amount of our present reality is dictated by our previous actions, choices and reactions.

(b) We have chosen (as souls) to learn certain "lessons" at each stage of our evolutionary process.

— If we have chosen to learn self-acceptance, it is natural to experience rejection from others so that we can develop inner self-worth.

— If we have chosen to develop self-confidence, we will naturally have chosen to experience an absence of external support.

— If we have chosen to learn forgiveness and unconditional love, we will have made a secret "soul agreement" with others to harm us so that we can then develop that type of forgiveness and love.

(c) Our present conscious and subconscious beliefs are perhaps the greatest cause of our preset reality. We attract to ourselves behaviours, events and life situations, which in some way "mirror" or "vibrate sympathetically" with how we think and feel in the present. Our present positive and negative conscious and subconscious beliefs, desires, needs, expectations and emotions such as fear, guilt, shame, love, peace and anger all combine to attract to us a corresponding external (and certainly internal) reality.

(d) In addition to attracting certain realities, we also interpret what is happening according to our beliefs. We give greater or lesser importance to specific issues and thus allow them to affect our state of mind to a greater or lesser degree. When we give great importance to our appearance or to how others perceive us or behave towards us, then our reality will change greatly every time we receive an input concerning our appearance or what others think.

Of these four factors we have control over only the last two at this point in time. We cannot change our past choices and our soul lessons are an integral part of our presence in these bodies. Thus we are left with changing our present conscious and subconscious beliefs. Firstly this will allow us to attract more positive behaviours, events and situations toward our being. Secondly, we will perceive life more positively so that even when we are not getting our preferred reality we feel secure, worthy and free to be our selves. This is our point of power. It is changing what we believe about life, others and most important of all, ourselves.

Some of those alternative ways of perceiving life will be described in this series.

Some of them are:

1. We alone are responsible for our lives, health and happiness as individuals and as a group.
2. We have the inner power and resourcefulness to deal with whatever life brings us.
3. Our self-worth is a function of our inner being and has nothing to do with appearance, affluence, position, knowledge or what others think.

4. Life is always giving us exactly what we need to create happiness and to continue our evolutionary process.
5. We are free to live our lives according to our own inner ideals and goals and to change our reality if we chose to.
6. We deeply love and seek to help our loved ones, while simultaneously remembering they are souls in the process of evolution who have chosen heir specific lessons.
7. We are all eternal souls in the evolutionary process of rediscovering and manifesting our inner divine nature.
8. Each being is divine creation and deserves our love and respect—including us.
9. Our life purpose is to individually and collectively transform our reality into a more enlightened and loving one.
10. Our basic lesson is Love.
11. All of this universe is an expression of the one Universal Omnipresent and Omnipotent Being — Consciousness.
12. We as co-creators with the Divine have been created to bless, spiritualise and transform the material world.

8

Power and Benefits of Positive Attitude

A good definition of "positive attitude" will emphasise being affirmative and certain, without being overconfident or intolerant. One comic definition of positive is "mistaken at the top of one's voice". A positive attitude is tolerant and forgiving of others. Any mental attitude that demands absolute acceptance by others is not positive—it is unproductive and negative.

Another element of a positive attitude is having a worthwhile goal or vision. The focus of your thoughts will determine what you will produce. Having "positive" thoughts about a goal that takes advantage of others in a negative way will not produce positive results. By using a just and fair approach to creating and maintaining goals, positive thinking will naturally fall in line with the goal or vision.

Creating a positive attitude takes work. The negative influence of other people, disappointment and failure all contribute to the sad fact that most people have only a limited positive attitude. Hard work and a commitment to persistence in staying positive are necessary. Learning and practising specific skills in increasing your positive thinking and protecting yourself from negative thinking is the challenge you must accept.

Maintaining a positive attitude comes from successful experience and a willingness to exercise will-power over the negative influences in life and in other people. Being influenced by negative forces takes no work at all. Negative influences come naturally and stay by repeatedly thinking about them. The duty of every person who chooses to make a positive attitude an unbreakable habit is to learn to stop negative thinking as soon as it begins. Replacing negative thoughts and influences with positive thoughts and feelings becomes easier and easier with practice.

A positive attitude is clearly more than just smiling and saying positive things. A true positive attitude comes from building habits that lead to success and away from surrender of control. The only thing in life we have absolute control over is our thoughts and our attitudes. Be willing to accept that fact and take control of your inner life. Make a positive attitude your strongest habit of thinking.

A positive attitude comes from observational learning in the environment and is partially achieved when a vision of good natured change in the mind is applied toward people, circumstances, events, or behaviours. Since it is difficult to quantify (measure) the effects of a positive mental attitude, it can be considered a philosophy and a way to approach life.

Positive thinking is a discipline that trains the human mind to change a perceived reality by repeatedly making positive mental statements. A person practices positive thinking when they derive a positive sense of well-being, optimism, belonging, meaning and/or purpose from being part of and contributing back to something larger and more permanent than themselves. Positive thinking is a process of choosing positive emotions from stimuli in the environment and applying them to perceptions and beliefs. The objective is to create an outlook that translates into a new or better chosen reality.

SUCCESS THROUGH A POSITIVE MENTAL ATTITUDE

The practice of positive thinking, repeated positive statements, and witnessing success through a positive mental attitude, is an idea many mystics and spiritual teachers have presented throughout history. Retiring certain emotions and breaking the addiction of old emotional states is a choice and requires persistent effort. A successful mental attitude that includes thoughts of gratitude, unconditional love, and freedom can translate into new perceptions of a person's perceived reality.

Adopting positive thinking with the intention of experiencing change can be accomplished in a number of ways:

- Recognise that change is needed.
- Believe change is possible. The brain can be re-programmed to provide support in your life.
- Give yourself permission to be in control of your own life.
- Practice awareness of your emotional state. Your internal state is what creates your external world.
- Release past negative experiences and move forward.
- Let go of self-criticism and move forward when a challenge arises.
- Stay in present moment thinking and affirm powerful and positive thoughts regularly.
- Practice verbal harmlessness. Identify and eliminate negative speech habits e.g., I can't, I'll try, or I've never been able to.
- Be thankful for what you have.
- Have a positive vision for your life and for others around you.

— Live proactively.
— Know that you are composed of unlimited Divine Spirit and are an example of uniqueness and wonder.

Positive thinking is associated with empowerment because an empowered thinker is one who masters their emotions and outlook on life. By being aware of our internal state, and how that translates into our reactions and behaviours, it is possible to develop the mind to support who we want to be, rather than being an effect of our world.

Positive attitude helps to cope more easily with the daily affairs of life. It brings optimism into your life, and makes it easier to avoid worry and negative thinking. If you adopt it as a way of life, it will bring constructive changes into your life, and makes them happier, brighter and more successful. With a positive attitude you see the bright side of life, become optimistic and expect the best to happen. It is certainly a state of mind that is well worth developing and strengthening.

Positive attitude manifests in the following ways:

— Positive thinking.
— Constructive thinking.
— Creative thinking.
— Expecting success.
— Optimism.
— Motivation to accomplish your goals.
— Being inspired.
— Choosing happiness.
— Not giving up.
— Looking at failure and problems as blessings in disguise.

- Believing in yourself and in your abilities.
- Displaying self-esteem and confidence.
- Looking for solutions.
- Seeing opportunities.

A positive attitude leads to happiness and success and can change your whole life. If you look at the bright side of life, your whole life becomes filled with light. This light affects not only you and the way you look at the world, but also your whole environment and the people around you. If it is strong enough, it becomes contagious.

The benefits of a positive attitude:

- Helps achieving goals and attaining success.
- Success achieved faster and more easily.
- More happiness.
- More energy.
- Greater inner power and strength.
- The ability to inspire and motivate yourself and others.
- Fewer difficulties encountered along the way.
- The ability to surmount any difficulty.
- Life smiles at you.
- People respect you.

If you have been exhibiting a negative attitude and expecting failure and difficulties, it is now the time to change the way you think. It is time to get rid of negative thoughts and behaviour and lead a happy and successful life. Why not start today? If you have tried and failed, it only means that you have not tried enough.

Power of Positive Attitude

Positive attitude, positive thinking, and optimism are now

known to be a root cause of many positive life benefits—the good life and well being. You'll live longer and be healthier and happier with a positive attitude toward life. In addition, you're more likely to be successful. Learn to use the power of thinking positive, adopting positive attitudes, and affirmations to gain important life benefits.

Attitude is a mental position relative to a way of thinking or being; a leaning toward that which you believe. A positive attitude is, therefore, the inclination to generally be in an optimistic, hopeful state of mind.

A positive attitude and optimistic thinking early in life predict health and well-being in later years. Analysis of 99 Harvard graduates found a strong correlation between their optimistic thinking as college students and good health at age 40 and above.

In his ground-breaking book, *A Primer in Positive Psychology*, Christopher Petersen, PhD, says, "...optimism has demonstrable benefits, and pessimism has drawbacks." He goes on to say, "...optimism...has been linked to positive mood and good morale; to perseverance and effective problem solving; to academic, athletic, military, occupational, and political success; to popularity; to good health; and even to long life and freedom from trauma." Even if you have been a pessimistic, negative thinker for many years, it's not too late to change your way of thinking and reap the benefits of a positive attitude.

Optimists believe they are accountable for good things and that good things will generally come their way. If something bad comes instead, optimists tend to write it off as an isolated incident, an anomaly, or something out of their control; optimists believe things will be better in the future.

If you're a person whose first thoughts about the meaning of something that's happened are negative thoughts, be encouraged by the knowledge that the first step toward a positive attitude and positive thinking is to simply think another thought. Thoughts are under your control. Your pessimistic way of thinking is habit; habits can be changed.

When you catch yourself thinking a pessimistic thought about an event in your life, first evaluate the evidence. What are the facts—not the fears—but the facts? Next, think of alternate explanations and future outcomes. When your old car suddenly makes a strange noise you may jump to the pessimistic conclusion that repair will be costly, but maybe a minor repair will solve the problem.

How to Develop a Positive Attitude?

Your thoughts and emotions, day in day out, affect all aspects of your life. Learning to be mindful of your "internal dialogue" will help you recognise thought patterns and how they may be affecting the way you handle the situations of daily living.

Many people have found that, when they tune in to their internal dialogue, much of it is negative. Thoughts like, "I could never do that" and "What if I fail?" can seriously impact the way you behave. The stress associated with attachment to this negative internal dialogue, in turn, affects every aspect of your life.

When we are stressed, certain hormones are produced by the body. When released infrequently, these hormones are harmless but, when produced continuously, they can cause serious damage. Cardiovascular disease is caused in part by the continuous bombardment of stress hormones and by the arterial damage caused by the free radicals created in the process.

Letting go of attachment to these negative thoughts and emotions is very self-liberating. This is a process in itself; however, well worth the effort.

Here are some ways to help you develop a more positive attitude and better manage the stressors in your life:

— *Listen to internal dialogue.* Divide one or more sheets of paper into two columns and, for a few days, jot down in the left column all the negative thoughts that come into your head. Rewrite each thought in a positive way in the second column. Practice doing this in your mind until it becomes a habit. (For example, "I'll never get this finished by the end of the day!" could become, "I will probably get most of this finished by the end of the day.")

— *Learn to communicate.* Not saying the things we feel can lead to a sense of frustration, hurt, anger or anxiety. If you find communicating difficult, or are afraid of arguments or bruised feelings, take a course in communicating effectively always having the intent of non-harm.

— *Get back to basics.* Reconnect with old friends, take the dog for a walk, visit an art gallery or listen to your favourite music. Enjoy a long, relaxing bath, read a great book, tell your child a story, or ask an older relative to tell you one! The simplest things in life give us the most pleasure.

— *Help someone out.* The simple act of helping others (humans, animals or Nature in general) helps us to feel joy. Pick up groceries for an aging neighbour, volunteer at your local hospital or read a book to someone with failing eyesight. If you are unsure of how to help out in your community, call your nearest volunteer centre.

- *Find your spirituality.* Research has shown that those who have developed their spirituality through associating with other spiritual individuals or having their own personal mindful beliefs, live longer, more satisfying lives. The secret is practising those beliefs, either through organised worship, or simple meditation in a quiet place.
- *Allow yourself to be loved.* The ability to love and be loved is the most basic human trait. We, as a society, have become disconnected from this most basic need—fear-based emotions (depression, loneliness, guilt, attachment and anger are the symptoms). Finding ways to reconnect with others is extremely helpful in developing a positive attitude.
- *Allow yourself to laugh and find humour in the simplest of things.* Laughter is a powerful mood elevator. If you are feeling down, read some jokes, watch a funny movie or just act "silly" once in a while. At times, it is a good thing to let yourself see the world through a child's eyes.
- *Participate in new physical and mental activities to improve confidence levels and coping mechanisms.* Building confidence could be as easy as learning the meanings of new words, learning about new topics or if you are right-handed using instead your left hand more frequently (left hand connects with more spiritual, intuitive and creative right side of the brain).
- *Follow the principles of holistic health*—enlightened body, speech and mind in harmony (better nutrition and exercise help improve mood and attitude).
- *Learn to communicate your needs more effectively.* For example, instead of using common language of

subordination expressed by such words as "no", "don't", "should", "stop", "good", "bad" and "have", you could instead try expressing your needs by stating "I need you to...". This peaceful language expresses needs and does not judge.

How to Maintain Positive Attitude

Is maintaining a positive attitude easier said than done? There are many times in our lives when putting on a smiley face is not easy and it may not even be what we want to do at that moment.

Think of when someone annoys you and you feel anger inside, perhaps even revengeful; or when you are busy with a project that doesn't seem to have given results for a long time, and you feel discouraged; or when you see people suffering that you can do nothing for, and the hopeless feeling.

This kind of situations bring up negative feelings, and then we cling on to them most of the times, specially if our ego is involved—like when you believe that someone has been unfair or rude to you and you feel you deserve an apology. Focusing on these negative thoughts only creates a circle in which the more you think about them, and feel negative, the more it seems that this is indeed reality.

The more you see the reality as being aggressive towards you, the more you feel bad about yourself. The best thing for you is to take a step back, say No to all those negative feelings, and choose to focus on the positive aspects in your life.

The following tips for maintaining a positive attitude could be the help you were looking for, in order to do that. You may be able to apply only one or maybe many of these tips to your current situation, and they may even inspire you to look for your own ways of feeling good about yourself. Use these tips to help you keep a positive attitude when things around you make you feel negative. Don't let discouragement, anger or sadness get you down any longer!

1. *Do something nice for yourself*: Take a warm bath, enjoy a walk on your own, spend an afternoon doing something that you like (reading, watching a good movie, playing an instrument, cooking, gardening). By focusing on yourself and taking some time off just for you, you put your negative circumstances and feelings aside for a while. When you come back, it's easier to deal with them, as you'll do it from a positive state of mind.
2. *Be grateful for what you already have:* Think sometimes that there are many people in wore situations than you are right now. This story went like "I complained that I had no shoes, until I saw a man with no feet". Realise that you receive things, people, and experiences into your life that other people have no access to, due to different reasons. Feel grateful for what you do have.
3. *Turn your attention outwards:* Take some time to help someone. Give time, attention and support to somebody that needs it. You could give a hand to a friend or spend an afternoon helping out at a charity group, for instance. At times we think that our problems are really big when things aren't really all that bad. Getting out of your own reality will help you put things into perspective and deal with them better afterwards.
4. *Don't look at results but consider the whole process:* This is true if you're disappointed about a project, because we tend to focus on immediate results. Think that the no-results state is only temporary.

Look at what you are doing as a whole process. Your only job is planning the process well, so that in the end it brings you the results you expect. See it this way and you will find it easier to keep on the positive attitude.

5. *Trust that everything will be all right:* When everything else seems to fall apart, trusting that everything will be all right is the best exercise for your mind and soul. Feel the overwhelming calmness when you feel the trust. Maintaining a positive attitude is a good starting point to enjoy a great life.

Positive Attitude Increases Motivation

Have you ever heard the saying that attitude is everything? If you have, then you may know it to be true. While it can be difficult to be positive all the time, being an optimist has been linked to many things, including better health. Doctors will tell you that patients who are optimistic about treatment are those that always recover faster than those who are pessimistic. When you are positive, you can accomplish things that some may have thought were unrealistic. A positive attitude can help you build strong relationships as well as create increased motivation. If you have a goal in mind that you are having a hard time finding motivation to meet, try having a positive attitude. Although it may seem challenging at times, try these easy tips in order to be more positive each day.

Wake up Nicer

Your whole day really starts with waking up. If you want to have a more positive attitude, make sure you can wake up in a calm environment. Those with children know too well that this can be difficult. However, you can practice doing things in advance to prepare for the morning so everything will flow smoothly. For instance, try laying out everyone's clothing the night before. Pack lunches and stick them in the fridge as well. Do anything you can to make your morning a little easier. You will find that with the ease, you will be more apt to have a positive start to the day.

Wave at Your Neighbours

Although this seems a little old fashioned to some people, when you are leaving home, try to wave at your neighbours. Offering a little smile and a quick wave is a great way to spread your positive attitude to everyone around you.

Take Your Time

Be sure that you leave for work or school each morning in plenty of time to get to your destination. When people have to rush, they tend to become flustered. You will be more motivated in general if you give yourself enough time to accomplish tasks.

Eat Lunch

People who claim they are unmotivated are often those that eat poorly, never exercise, and work over 40 hours a week. When you are not taking care of yourself, it is difficult to stay positive and be motivated to do anything at all. Even the simplest tasks like laundry on the weekend can seem overwhelming. Be sure to eat healthy meals throughout the day and never skip lunch!

Socialise with Friends

Part of staying positive has to do with your personal relationships. If you are trying so hard to do as much as possible, then you probably have little time to socialise.

Take the time to socialise with friends as much as you can. This will help you stay positive and help your motivation continue.

Limit Media Influence

As informative as it can be, watching or reading too much media news coverage can be harmful to a positive person. The tragedy of it all is that the news is typically filled with depressing and over-dramatised events. The news crews choose the most dramatic things to put on the air or in print. Therefore, you are only seeing the worst of the worst. Try limiting yourself to this type of influence and you will be more positive altogether.

Pretend To Be Happy

One key trick to staying positive is to act positive even when you are feeling down. By acting like you are positive, you will find that you can lift your own spirits faster than anything else. Although it may seem like you are faking it, chances are no one will even know. The next time you are feeling down and not motivated, take on a positive attitude role and your motivation will come naturally with your character.

There are many things you can do in order to keep a positive attitude throughout your days. These are minor changes in your day and in your attitude that can be done daily in order to train yourself to be a more positive person. When you are a more positive person you will be a more motivated person. This will all lead to a more successful life.

Self-motivation and positive attitude are almost intertwined. A positive attitude is a prerequisite to self-motivation and therefore it is essential that if one wants to stay motivated at all times one should adopt a positive mental attitude.

However, attaining a positive attitude is not easy. It requires you to be in a state of general happiness, which can be attained only if you are at peace with yourself.

Man has tried to 'find happiness' for years. But it is ironical that he searches for this happiness in places far and wide while it can be found only within oneself. The real search for happiness starts by looking 'inside' and understanding the real purpose of ones life. It is important to realise the happiness is relative in nature and that while some find it in work, achievement and success, others find it in love, relationships and family ties, affectionate friendships and in faith.

It is also important to understand that is one tries to seek happiness in external material gains or even in external manifestations of love from others, there is only disappointment to be found. The main idea is to accept your strengths, weaknesses, capabilities, situation and life as it is. Complete acceptance of the situation leads to a feeling of contentment and happiness at what you have.

A positive perspective towards all events in life can lead to happiness and emotional wellness. As the saying goes, "I was pining about the fact that I did not have shoes, when I saw a man without feet".

However, all of the above does not mean that you should lead yourself to total contentment and complacency. It is necessary that you dissociate your happiness from the daily efforts that you need to make to make your life better. By all means, set material objectives for yourself and do everything in your scope to make them possible. But do not allow the success of these efforts to rule your overall attitude and well-being.

Over time, you will realise that it is this positive attitude and the ability to motivate yourself under any circumstances that aids you in the process of achieving your goals. Optimism can break the dismal ropes of negativity and rationalism and can help you accomplish tasks that otherwise seem impossible. A positive attitude can help you take failure in your stride.

When you are 'happy' and have a positive attitude, you do not need to rely on external motivation to achieve and accomplish goals. On the other hand, in the absence of self-motivation, initial spurts in motivation caused by external sources, tend to wear off after the initial euphoria.

A spiritual understanding of life, a positive attitude, proper perspective of the events of life can help you achieve a continuous state of motivation. Such a high level of self-motivation can stand the test of mood swings, transient depression or failures.

Benefits of Positive Attitudes

The benefits of positive thinking and positive attitude are well documented. Researchers of Positive Psychology find that people with positive attitudes are happier, healthier, and live longer than those with negative attitudes and habitual negative thinking.

A positive attitude is simply an inclination or leaning toward the positive aspects of any situation. Thinking positively is not putting one's head in the sand, nor is it being unrealistic. A positive attitude recognises the negative aspects of a situation, but chooses to focus instead on the hope and opportunity available within every situation.

What are you to do if you seem inclined to focus on the negative? Even though you may be pre-disposed to negative thinking due to genetics or your childhood environment, you can learn to move your thinking to the positive side. Learning to use positive affirmations will help, as will sharpening your awareness to nip negative thinking in the bud before it escalates. Learning to question and re-structure your thinking when it turns negative will help you think positively more often and stay that way.

If you are wondering what are the benefits of positive attitude, then you are on the right track. You are already thinking positively and you are searching and learning. And that's wonderful. One of the biggest benefits of positive attitude is stress relief. Yes, thinking positively leads to a more peaceful you.

Experts recognise that negative thoughts are one of the causes of stress. Stress is a natural part of life and everyone experiences it. However, how you respond to stress, determines the impact it has on you.

Have you ever noticed how some people bounce back quickly after experiencing a stressful event? One of the reasons is their attitude. They do not dwell on the negative, but they look for the positive.

Stress is often defined as our reaction to an event. For example, two people are laid off from a job.

One person says:"I am not happy about loosing my income, but it's a good opportunity for me to start my own online business".

Another person says: "This is terrible, I will never find another job, this my end".

Who do you think will experience less stress from this event? You are right. The person who found something positive in the situation.

Other benefits of positive attitude are:

— More happiness and joy in life.

— Improved self-esteem and self-image.

— Improved relationships with family and friends.

— More closeness and intimacy.

- More success at work, school, or with hobbies and sports.
- Increased motivation.
- More energy.
- Improved sense of well-being.

One step towards cultivating a positive attitude is developing gratitude. When you focus on what you have, your outlook automatically changes. It is impossible to be grateful and negative at the same time.

9

Improve Yourself with Positive Affirmations

Every thought you think every word you say is an affirmation All of our self-talk or inner dialogue is a stream of affirmations. We are continually affirming subconsciously with our words and thoughts and this flow of affirmations is creating our life experience in every moment. Our beliefs are just learned thought patterns that we have developed since childhood, many of these work well for us, but others may now be working against us, they are dysfunctional and may be sabotaging us from achieving what we believe we want. Every affirmation we think or say is a reflection of our inner truth or beliefs. It is important to realise that many of these "inner truths" may not actually be true for us now or may be based on invalid or inappropriate impressions we constructed as children, which if examined as an adult can be exposed as inappropriate.

Our subconscious uses the behaviour patterns we have learned to automatically respond and react to many everyday events in our life. This is essential to our survival, we need to be able to respond quickly to events around us which would be impossible if we had to re-examine every aspect of things every time something simple happens. Our learned responses and thought patterns enable us to automatically respond to circumstances quickly and easily. Problems arise however, if at an early stage some of the foundation beliefs on which many of the others are built were formed from a skewed perspective, maybe the strategy was appropriate for a perceived difficult circumstance, however often such beliefs are totally inappropriate for succeeding in the real world as adults.

You can use "positive affirmations", which are usually short positive statements targeted at a specific subconscious set of beliefs, to challenge and undermine negative beliefs and to replace them with positive self-nurturing beliefs. It is a kind of "brainwashing" only you get to choose which negative beliefs to wash away. The way these statements are constructed is extremely important. It is important to remember of course that everything we say and think is a positive affirmation, using positive affirmation statements forces us to keep focussed on our inner goals and reminds us to think consciously about our words and thoughts and to modify them to reflect our positive affirmation.

An affirmation can be any simple statement. It is something positive that is phrased in the present tense. A good example of an affirmation would be: "I am strong" or "I am beautiful" or even "I am not fat". There are multitudes of lists of affirmations that are available online and elsewhere. However, affirmations have proven to be ineffective most of the time, because people do not utilise them consistently or long enough for their brains to be able to absorb it. Also, they make the common mistake of using the conscious part of the brain, where a filter, like a pre-dominant insecurity, can hinder the input of these affirmations.

Subliminal affirmations do not have much difference from regular affirmations however they are delivered in such a way that you can barely detect or recognise it. For example, a message can just appear as a quick flash on your screen. Even if you didn't quite catch what it was, you can be assured that your subconscious mind picked up every single flash and recognises exactly what it said.

These kinds of affirmations can even be sent to you through your speakers. The audio is sent at a non-regular frequency that is below hearing level. This enables your subconscious mind to receive these messages instead of getting them through your conscious mind.

The subconscious mind is a truly amazing thing. Out of your total brain mass, it occupies about 83% of it and controls 96-98% of your total behaviour and perception. Just imagine that! On the other hand, your conscious mind is out of focus every 6-8 seconds or so, whilst your subconscious mind is never out of focus! Your conscious mind may retain information and then lose it after a few seconds, but your subconscious mind retains all the information that it gets and never loses it.

The conscious mind can process approximately 2,000 bits of data per second. Quite a number, isn't it? But hear this, the subconscious mind can process 400 billion bits of data per second and retains all of it and loses none!

How then can you benefit from this? A habit is formed by simply taking a thought of action and thinking it over and over again. This thought will eventually become a habit, and with continued repetition, it will then become a belief or an attitude. This means you can change these beliefs just by simply frequently and repeatedly imprinting your new or desired belief on your subconscious mind. So if you have a bad habit that you want to replace with a good one, just think about it continuously and you can eventually eliminate that bad habit and enforce the good one. This is the marvellous work of subliminal affirmations.

Uses of Positive Affirmations

You will be hard pushed to find any self-help programme anywhere that does not include affirmations, even the ones that appear to pooh-pooh affirmations include them under some slightly different guise. And the reason for this is, they work. The more determined you are to make your changes, the more you are prepared to accept change and let go of the past, the better they will work for you.

By choosing to think and say positive affirmations as true, the subconscious is forced into one of two reactions—avoidance or reappraisal. The bigger the issue the bigger the gap between the positive affirmation and the perceived inner truth and the more likely that one is going to experience resistance. This is where the subconscious finds it easier to stay with its perceived inner truth and avoid the challenge using any means at its disposal to avoid examining the issue. You will recognise this reaction by a strong negative feeling inside as you state the positive affirmations.

Equally, if your experience a sense of joy and well-being, your mind is instinctively responding to something it believes to be true. When you get this emotion, you know your affirmations are working!

Continually repeating affirmations with conviction and passion will chip away at even the strongest resistance. However there are a number of additional techniques you can use that will super-charge your affirmations and magnify their effectiveness many fold. The effect can be startling and things can change very quickly as the dysfunctional beliefs get identified and replaced by your own new inner truth.

Depending on how deep into your consciousness these beliefs lay, every other learned pattern and belief that relied on the original belief as a premise, becomes unfounded. The subconscious has to re-examine them all, this can lead to a period of introspection.

Because affirmations actually reprogramme your thought patterns, they change the way you think and feel about things, and because you have replaced dysfunctional beliefs with your own new positive beliefs, positive change comes easily and naturally. This will start to reflect in your external life, you will start to experience seismic changes for the better in many aspects of your life.

From day one, there will be affirmations you love and enjoy saying, these affirmations are likely to be very effective for you and you are likely to start experience changes almost immediately. Others will feel very negative, almost like a big lie, this indicates resistance and these areas may take longer to impact. How quickly you can resolve an issue like this is like asking how long is a piece of string. It depends on the issue, how deeply the belief is held and how determined you are to bring about change in that area of your life, the latter being perhaps the most important of all.

If you are truly ready and want to make changes, the quicker those changes will come for you. People have made cognitive changes in their beliefs almost instantaneously, once you are prepared to embrace and accept a change and you believe it to be right for you from your very heart, then that change will happen. So it is not really a question of time, more a question of how accepting of change you can be.

Our free affirmation programme uses affirmations extensively to target negative thought patterns, it runs for a minimum three months during which time if you have done everything we would definitely expect you to have started experiencing positive changes.

However, you should be under no illusion that by embarking on this process you are starting a journey for your lifetime. As you see and experience the techniques working for yourself will be driven to explore your inner-self further and other techniques. As you make your changes in one aspect of your life, other issues will pop up that you may want to deal with. The joy is, you would now have the knowledge and skill to deal with these issues effectively.

No matter what aspect of life you're dealing with or who you are, affirmations will not only make you feel better about yourself and your life. But if used correctly, they can manifest real change in your life. Changing the way you think, reprogramming your mind and removing the old negative beliefs that have been sabotaging you again and again throughout your life. They can enable you to achieve the life you've always wanted for yourself!

Nearly 90% of our thoughts are negative, no wonder we find ourselves struggling. Each negative thought or word is a negative affirmation and these nasty little beasts can be even more powerful than positive affirmations because we often find them easier to accept. It is these negative thoughts that feed and validate our negative internal beliefs. Under this kind of negative bombardment most people simply do not have the strength to break free of their negative thoughts and become hopelessly locked into their own (usually false) negative beliefs.

Positive affirmations are designed to challenge those negative beliefs and start to stem the flow of negative thoughts and words that seek to validate them. Affirmations are more than just repeating words. It is a whole process of becoming aware of your thoughts and words in everyday life, choosing to think and project happy positive thoughts. The more you can consciously inject the spirit of you affirmations into your daily thoughts and words, the quicker they will work for you.

Creating Your Own Affirmations

Start by taking some time to think about areas in your life you would like to improve and how you might want your life to be. It is worth taking some time over this process. Write the most important ones down in a list.

Now look at each item on the list and write out a few positive statements for each. They must be positive and in the present tense, focus on what you do want, not on what you don't want.

Creating your own affirmations is the perfect way to get the right affirmations for you. They should give you a good idea on how they should look and feel.

Some example affirmations for some common issues are.

1. *Affirmations for health:*
   - Every Cell in my body vibrates with energy and health.
   - Loving myself heals my life. I nourish my mind, body and soul.
   - My body heals quickly and easily.
2. *Affirmations for abundance*:
   - I prosper wherever I turn and I know that I deserve prosperity of all kinds.
   - The more grateful I am, the more reasons I find to be grateful.
   - I pay my bills with love as I know abundance flows freely through me.

3. *Affirmations for love:*
   - I know that I deserve Love and accept it now.
   - I give out Love and it is returned to me multiplied.
   - I rejoice in the Love I encounter everyday.
4. *Affirmations for romance:*
   - I have a wonderful partner and we are both happy and at peace.
   - I release any desperation and allow love to find me.
   - I attract only healthy relationships.
5. *Affirmations for weight loss*
   - I am the perfect weight for me.
   - I choose to make positive healthy choices for myself.
   - I choose to exercise regularly.
6. *Affirmations for self-esteem*
   - When I believe in myself, so do others.
   - I express my needs and feelings.
   - I am my own unique self—special, creative and wonderful.
7. *Affirmations for peace and harmony*
   - All my relationships are loving and harmonious.
   - I am at peace.
   - I trust in the process of life.
8. *Affirmations for joy and happiness*
   - Life is a joy filled with delightful surprises.
   - My life is a joy filled with love, fun and friendship all I need do is stop all criticism, forgive, relax and be open.

— I choose love, joy and freedom, open my heart and allow wonderful things to flow into my life.

9. *Common Positive Affirmations:*
   — I am healthy and happy.
   — Wealth is pouring into my life.
   — I am sailing on the river of wealth.
   — I am getting wealthier each day.
   — My body is healthy and functioning in a very good way.
   — I have a lot of energy.
   — I study and comprehend fast.
   — My mind is calm.
   — I am calm and relaxed in every situation.
   — My thoughts are under my control.
   — I radiate love and happiness.
   — I am surrounded by love.
   — I have the perfect job for me.
   — I am living in the house of my dreams.
   — I have good and loving relations with my wife/husband.
   — I have a wonderful and satisfying job.
   — I have the means to travel abroad, whenever I want to.
   — I am successful in whatever I do.
   — Everything is getting better every day.
   — I can be a winner.
   — I am the best friend I have.
   — I have solved problems like this before.

— I have the ability to handle this.
— I am a capable human being.
— I deserve to love and to be loved.
— I am a skilful and artistic person.
— I can show others a good example.
— Letting go is best for them and for me.
— They will thank me in the future.
— Nothing is worth losing my sanity over.
— I am responsible only for my own feelings.
— I owe no one explanations for my behaviour, which is legally, morally, and ethically correct.
— I deserve to have my rights recognised.
— I am a deserving human being.
— I deserve to enjoy the fruits of my labour.
— I deserve to be rewarded for what I do.
— I love myself for who I am.
— It is OK to be selfish if I don't hurt anyone.
— I like the way I handle problems.
— I am able to handle any problem I face.
— I have the right to feel the way I do.
— My children will benefit from my healthy changes.
— My children will survive my healthy changes.
— My family will benefit from my relaxing more.
— I deserve to relax more and take it easy.
— There are beautiful things happening in my life daily.
— I experience the excitement of growth daily.
— Change is a blessing I am working toward.

- Taking risks is the path to growth.
- I grow in love daily.
- I face each new day as a race to be won.
- I am winning in the race of life.
- I am a rich treasure ready to be found.
- Let others know who I am.
- Say hello to a new person today.
- Open up to be loved today.
- Be responsible. Relax!

Supercharging Affirmations

There are other techniques you can use that can supercharge the effectiveness of your affirmations. Perhaps the most powerful way of using affirmations is to state them whilst looking in the mirror. Some of the most important messages you have received have been from people looking you straight in the eye. By looking yourself in the eye as you state your affirmation you magnify the importance of the message to yourself.

Written Affirmations

A great way of keeping your affirmation at the forefront of your mind is to write them down, leave notes or cards around so that you notice them throughout the day.

Say Affirmations with Passion

Say your affirmations with passion, the higher your emotional state as you say them, the more effective they are.

Sing or Chant Affirmations

One of the most effective ways to use affirmations is to sing them! The mind is much more accepting of affirmation messages when they are sung. If you have ever attended a Louise Hay "Heal your life Workshop", this technique is used extensively.

Subliminal Affirmations

There are a number of techniques that attempt to by-pass the conscious mind and its resistance by transmitting the affirmations to you subliminally. There are a number of books available that include subliminal affirmations, the trouble with this technology is that it often comes unsupported and people expect it to simply work without doing anything for themselves. There is however a very powerful technique known as an "affirmation bath". This is often used in workshops because it requires several people sitting around a person making positive statements about them. An affirmation bath is a truly amazing experience, the multiple voices, coming from multiple directions, often simultaneously simply overwhelm the minds ability to resist what is being said and the positive affirmations slip straight through to the subconscious. It is normally impossible to experience this unless you can get a group of like minded people together or you attend a workshop.

Power of Affirmations

Affirmations are positive statements that describe a desired situation, and which are repeated many times, in order to impress the subconscious mind and trigger it into positive action. In order to ensure the effectiveness of the affirmations, they have to be repeated with attention, conviction, interest and desire.

Imagine that you are swimming with your friends in a swimming pool. They swim fifteen rounds, something you have never done before, and desiring to win the respect of your friends, you want to show them that you can make it too. You start swimming, and at the same time keep repeating in your mind, "I can do it, I can do it...". You keep thinking and believing that you are going to complete the fifteen rounds. What are you actually doing? You are repeating positive affirmations.

More than often, people repeat in their minds negative words and statements concerning the situations and events in their lives, and consequently bring upon themselves undesirable situations. Words and statements work both ways, to build or destroy. It is the way we use them that determines whether they are going to bring good or harmful results.

Often, people repeat negative statements in their minds, without even being aware of what they are doing. Do you keep thinking and telling yourself that you cannot do something, that you are too lazy, lack inner strength or that you are going to fail? Your subconscious mind accepts as true what you keep saying, and eventually attracts corresponding events and situations into your life, irrespective whether they are good or bad for you, so why not choose only positive statements?

Affirmations programme the mind in the same way commands and scripts programme a computer. They work in the same manner as creative visualisation. The repeated words help you focus your mind on your aim, and automatically build corresponding mental images in the conscious mind, which affect the subconscious mind. The conscious mind, the mind you think with, starts this process, and then the subconscious mind takes charge. By using this process consciously and intently, you can affect your subconscious mind and thereby transform your habits, behavior, mental attitude and reactions, and even reshape your external life.

Sometimes results appear quickly, but often more time is required. Depending on your goal, sometimes you might attain immediate results, and sometimes it might take days, weeks, months or more. Getting results depends on several factors, such as the time, focus, faith and feelings you invest in repeating your affirmations, on the strength of your desire, and on how big or small is your goal. It is important to understand that repeating positive affirmations for a few minutes, and then thinking negatively the rest of the day, neutralises the effects of the positive words. You have to refuse thinking negative thoughts, if you wish to attain positive results.

How to Repeat Affirmations?

It is advisable to repeat affirmations that are not too long, as they are easier to remember. Repeat them anytime your mind is not engaged in something in particular, such as while travelling in a bus or a train, waiting in line, walking etc, but do not affirm while driving or crossing a street. You may also repeat them in special sessions of 5-10 minutes each, several times a day.

Relax any physical, emotional or mental tension while affirming. The stronger the concentration, the more faith you have in what you are doing, the more feelings you put into the act, the stronger and faster will be the results.

Choose only positive words, describing what you really want. If you desire to lose weight, do not tell yourself "I am not fat" or "I am losing weight." These are negative statements, bringing into the mind mental images of what you do not want. Say instead, "I am getting slim" or "I have reached my right weight". Such words evoke positive images in the mind.

Always affirm in the present tense, not the future tense. Saying, "I will be rich", means that you intend to be rich one day, in the indefinite future, but not now. It is more effective to say, and also feel, "I am rich now", and the subconscious mind will work overtime to make this happen now, in the present. The power of affirmations can help you to transform your life.

How Positive Affirmations Change Your Life?

Positive affirmations are effective and beneficial tools for improving self-esteem because these statements are positive, tangible energies that, by redirecting our thoughts, can alter our emotions. Perhaps, you may not have realised it but the things you tell yourself and the beliefs you have about yourself contribute in a concrete way to your self-esteem. If you are feeling inadequate and weak, it is most likely you believe that you are so, and very soon your belief will become fact. In like manner, you can increase your self-esteem by actively working on modifications to your self-talk and basic beliefs about yourself.

It is hard to think highly of yourself when you constantly bad-mouth yourself. Like a bad recording, the inner voice of your ego constantly gives subliminal feedback, and if you programme it with negative thoughts, it will keep saying you're never good enough and whittling away your self-esteem. With affirmations, you are able to drown out the negative chatter with positive statements, helping tremendously in improving self-esteem.

Positive affirmations have a direct instantaneous impact on the way we feel in each particular moment. They can have a remarkable influence on the overall quality our everyday life. Affirmations can certainly affect health and well-being as well. If you tend to dwell on statements such as "I am so depressed today. My life is a complete disaster." How does that kind of statement make you feel? Instead, put a completely different spin on your way of thinking, and state confidently "I choose to find joy in this moment" or "My life is improving every day, a little at time." Now, isn't that a much better-feeling statement? As you state an affirmation, really engage in the meaning of it, and connect with the positive feeling it evokes.

Bringing affirmations into your life is a process and may take some time to learn, but be open to the innate goodness that resides within you. Create your own affirmations to reflect this inner you. Start today — right now! As you are reading this, use this Affirmation, Attitude, Action: "I am worthy of peace, joy and abundance. I feel these flowing easily into my experience. I open myself to healing and happiness!"

For many people, they will decide to try to use affirmations to create these changes in their lives. And the use of an affirmation can help to produce changes, even very rapidly. However, you must realise that alone, an affirmation will not effect a great change in your life. You have to add action into the mix.

Just repeating a certain phrase or affirmative statement will not all of a sudden make you wealthy. And repeating a certain message will not magically melt pounds off of your body. What can and will happen, is that you can begin to change the way that you think about things. You can change your perspective. As a result, you will begin to take new actions, ones that are positive and more in line with what you want to experience.

Affirmations should become a part of your daily ritual. A more powerful choice would be to use them multiple times throughout the day to get the best effect. This way, you will be giving a constant new message for your mind to respond to. Your affirmations should also make you feel excited, passionate and full of energy to get the best results.

Other Books on

GENERAL

1.	Travel & Tourism An Industry Facilitator **(New)**	295/-
2.	World's Great Authors And Poets **(New)**	125/-
3.	Judgment: No Aircrash No Death **(New)**	250/-
4.	Smart House-Keeping for Modern Women **(New)**	125/-
5.	Develop Super Power Memory **(New)**	125/-
6.	World's Great Personalities **(New)**	125/-
7.	Personality Plus **(New)**	125/-
8.	Power of Positive Thinking **(New)**	125/-
9.	Art of Successful Parenting **(New)**	150/-
10.	A Handbook of Etiquettes **(New)**	125/-
11.	How to Beat Your Competitors **(New)**	125/-
12.	World's Great Scientists **(New)**	125/-
13.	How to Negotiate Effectively **(New)**	125/-
14.	The Kama Sutra of Mallinaga Vatsyayana **(New)**	125/-
15.	Vatsyayana's Kamasutra Select **(New)**	125/-
16.	Patriot: The Unique Indian Leader Netaji Subhas Chandra Bose	250/-
17.	Body Language	125/-
18.	Art of Successful Living	125/-
19.	Make Your Boss Happy	110/-
20.	Jokes for All	75/-
21.	Selected Dohas	295/-

22.	Baby Names for Girls **(New)**	85/-
23.	Baby Names for Boys **(New)**	85/-
24.	Art of Public Speaking	125/-
25.	The World's Greatest Speeches	125/-
26.	Group Discussions	95/-
27.	Personality Development	95/-
28.	Think Positive & Things Will Go Right	95/-
29.	Once in a Blue Moon (A Tantra Tale)	125/-
30.	God is Dead	125/-
31.	Travel India (A Complete Guide to Tourists)	295/-
32.	Glimpses of Urdu Poetry	350/-
33.	Indian Mythology (PB)	195/-
34.	Helpline for Stressed Parents	125/-
35.	Grow Rich with Peace of Mind	125/-
36.	How to be Fit & Young **(New)**	125/-
37.	How to Succeed in Life	125/-
38.	How to Reduce Tension	125/-
39.	A Book of Stenography	95/-
40.	Business Letters	95/-
41.	Baby Names for Boy	75/-
42.	Baby Names for Girl	75/-
43.	Indian National Congress	450/-

Lotus PRESS

4263/3, Ansari Road,
Darya Ganj, New Delhi-110002
Ph.: 32903912, 23280047,9811594448
E-mail: lotus_press@sify.com
www.lotuspress.co.in